MW00605521

Shop. Cook. Eat.

Katherine Frelon

To Charlie and Matilda.

The most delicious, sweetest,
perfect ingredients of all.

Published by Curran Pendleton Press dba Author's Boutique, Raleigh, NC.

All rights reserved. No part of this book may be reproduced in any form or by any electronic or mechanical means, without permission in writing from the authors. The only exception is by a reviewer, who may quote short excerpts in a review.

Copyright © 2014 Katherine Frelon

Cover image copyright © Curran Pendleton Press

Design by Benjamin Bennett. www.baar.co.uk

Main photography: Clive Bozzard-Hill. www.bozza-uk.com
Other photography: Ffotos by Ffion

No part of this book may be reproduced or transmitted in any form or by any means, electronic or mechanical, including photocopying, recording, or by any information storage and retrieval system, permitted by law. For information contact: Curran Pendleton Press dba Author's Boutique, Raleigh, NC.

Hardcover:
ISBN-10: 1941065007
ISBN-13: 978-1-941065-00-6

Paperback:
ISBN-10: 1941065015
ISBN-13: 978-1-941065-01-3

eBook:
ISBN-10: 1941065023
ISBN-13: 978-1-941065-02-0

Shop. Cook. Eat.

Katherine Frelon

CURRAN
PENDLETON
press

Acknowledgements

Writing this book has been, as I'm sure every new author will say, is a roller coaster of emotions! The basic process of putting pen to paper is a universal function we learn even before attending kindergarden, but to put a pen to paper and create something out of nothing takes time, imagination and nurturing.

My publisher, as we were driving to the UK from my Cookery School, talked about the emotional release of finally achieving publication from just a seed of an idea formed many years ago. She wasn't wrong!

But, through the sleepless nights, frantic cooking and recipe consistency I was never alone. Sherrie Wilkolaski was at my side, as was Benjamin Bennett – the international crusaders! Kept alive by Clive Bozzzard-Hill's magnificent photography, we plotted the pathway to Shop. Cook. Eat!

I have always been surrounded by friends and family that supported my crazy outrageous ideas, some of which worked, most of which didn't. One thing I have always been is consistent with working hard, remaining focused, often leading to the brink of girlie tears and always within an inch of the cliff!

Without their support in all its guises it would be impossible to achieve all that I have and for that I am truly blessed and eternally grateful!

In whatever situation, entertaining and taking care of my children, hiking cakes down a tow path to deliver to fairs, collecting forgotten ingredients in the middle of the night as I obsessively create a new recipe without first checking I had everything in the pantry!

It must be pointed out however, that they were always compensated by copious amounts of food testing but it could in no way repay their loyalty and belief in what I was trying to achieve.

So thank you, Darren & Lisa Hooper, Sara & Martin James, Gilly & Thierry Bresson, Lorna & Andrew Kirkwood, Mr Bob!, Sara, John & James Rowland, Karen Roberts, Lizzie Troup, Alison Goldingham, Sarah & David Praill, Alison Smallman, Mabel Jones.

All of my barging buddies who have coped with crazed
and frantic recipe creations, as they try and navigate through
locks with tagliatelli draped around the deck on one day
and yards of boudin blanc on another, I'm *so* sorry
I couldn't list everyone!

All the crew who have worked with me in both countries,
Brendan, Sharon, Romy, Roxanne, Nathaniel, Tor, Avril –
nothing to say but you are the best of the bunch!

To all of my clients without exception, Thank you! As
you are the reason I cook too. Your enthusiasm and passion
for food is intoxicating and you inspire me to search for
new recipes!

To the members of International Food Wine Travel Writers
Association, Luxbeat Magazine, Storm – my PR company
in London – and all of those who have professionally
supported me!

My Father and Linda who quietly watch form the sidelines
and pick up the pieces when the pressure is to great!

My Bro, who just shrugs his shoulders as if to say, 'of course
you can do it, what's the problem!'

Yannick who has been instrumental 'unknowingly' in
enabling me to pursue my dream by just being there to
pour the wine, cook the dinner, wrap me up in a blanket
with a hot water bottle as I sit for hours on end at the
computer or cook night and day for weeks on end!

To my Mother, Nana and most faithful, supportive and loyal
friend who look down from above, this would definitely not
be possible without you!

To the ultimate critics, my beautiful children Charlie and
Matilda, who, as so often happens, are always hungry
in a house full of food, but they find nothing to eat!
Sound familiar?!

To all the characters who have shared their family recipes
over the years, who've fed me from their precious food stores
and poured wine into my glass, Merci!

Foreword

Writing an introduction for *Shop. Cook. Eat.* is an unexpected delight, as Katherine Frelon brings joy into anyone's life who has the pleasure of meeting her.

Our trio of travel journalists had extended our barge trip to Burgundy and spent the late morning and afternoon wine tasting, while heading to la Ferme de la Lochère. We had no idea what to expect, as we had been in old buildings and tight quarters. When we stepped inside, it was sheer elegance and beauty, and none more so than exhibited by its host, Katherine. To say her personality matched the bubbles in our welcome champagne is not an understatement.

I'm personal friends with French Master Chef Hervé Laurent, and have met Paul Bocuse, Thomas Keller and Daniel Boulud among others, while attending Bocuse d'Or. But experiencing French cooking with a U.K. chef who relocated to France to embrace its culture was one of the highlights of my world travels. Since I've travelled so widely, I rarely single out a "highlight," but this occasion deserved it.

Since our initial visit, we have remained in touch, as Katherine's skills are desired worldwide. In addition to offering week-long classes at La Ferme de la Lochère, she frequently appears in the U.K. and Chateaux's throughout France to share her talent and skills. While she imparts her knowledge, Katherine is sure to immerse guests into the local culture. She has been a chef on barges and, as a result, has many clients in the U.S. Captivated by her talent and personality, they often fly her across the pond to work her magic in their kitchens for special events.

Her skill, energy and enthusiasm for life are contagious. When clients are with Katherine, they pick up her love and appreciation of food, life, family, culture and all that surrounds it.

If anyone feels uncomfortable in the kitchen, she will put them at ease. *Shop. Cook. Eat.* will introduce readers to Katherine and I know they'll feel like they've known her. While experiencing her journey, readers will learn and possibly decide they do want the pleasure of meeting her first hand.

Maralyn D. Hill

Introduction

"To invite a person to your house is to take charge of his happiness so long as he is beneath your roof. The mistress of the house should always be certain that the coffee be excellent; whilst the master should be answerable for the quality of his wines and liqueurs."

Isabella Beeton

Looking back over my childhood memories of 'Toad in the Hole,' 'Roast Beef and Yorkshire Pudding', 'Sponge Syrup and Custard,' and all things traditionally English, little did I think that one day I would be living in the wilds of rural France with the local livestock for neighbours!

How strange life can be!

Writing a cookbook however, has always been one of my greatest daydreams since first starting school. Composing poetry, stories and very, long letters to my Grandmother was a huge part of my life as a novice writer.

Being grammatically and literally challenged has not deterred me from writing recipes and ideas down for the past 30 years, on any scrap of paper that comes to hand. The best ones are still in use today, tucked behind the mustard pot, or poking out from under a saucepan lid, all covered in various sticky ingredients!

Around the same time that I started cooking at school my family started to travel across the waters to France. At the time, this was for me a far away, exotic place where they smoked strong cigarettes that stuck to their bottom lip enabling them to drink a slug of some strange aniseed liquid called Pastis, very early in the morning. Where most of the rural women wore the standard housecoat and the men blue jumpsuits. A strange and foreign lot that spoke not one word of English!

"What are we doing here?" I mulled to myself over and over again as our little old Renault, packed so tightly with our first ever second-hand tent, bumped painstakingly along the D roads towards our destination of St. Palais Sur Mer.

But as we turned the corner and the sight of the sea came into view so did the market! Voila! Now I understood. The vibrant colours of the veggie's, fragrant juicy summer fruits, earthy mushrooms picked that morning, sweet strawberries, freshly baked bread, fresh flowers it was totally overwhelming. There would be folk with grubby hands selling their vegetables freshly dug that morning, warm bread, amazing ripe cheeses; the list goes on and on.

As we went further through France ending up each year in Cannes, where the undercover market is one of my most

favourite sights, I knew I would have to make my home here. It just made me want to Cook! Now all these years later I am, and loving every minute of it. Let me share with you what helped me make the decision to follow my passion.

One day, in a rainy London rush hour night, when I'd just broken down on Battersea Bridge, tooting and shaking of heads ensued from commuters all around, break down truck, insurance, blah blah blah. Finally, in the wee small hours, I get back home to a county so far out of London it would probably be quicker to fly! So, calling it a day, a hot bath is the way forward, only there's no hot water and no wine! It was definitely time to make a change!

Here I am 25 years later and I have to say it does seem a bit surreal. You know the thing is when you follow your parents on vacation, you never really get a say in where you go, what you do or if there is anything that might actually interest you once you arrive.

I never studied French at school seriously, having moved to France 18 months before I arrived, I just found the whole grammar thing totally pointless!

Never in a million years did I ever think I would actually live in France, speaking it every day, even dreaming and writing half the shopping list in French. My written French is still pretty poor if the truth were known, far too long winded for me. I'd rather just tell it like it is, so much easier!

I think one of the main reasons I chose France was because it really is just across the water from the UK so my parents wouldn't be too upset about me leaving. Plus they'd get to come and stay whenever they liked, no more camp sites. Yeah! I also felt naturally drawn to a country that still maintains a culture and tradition centred around family values, and a natural flair for throwing a great party at every possible opportunity.

But, unlike my own crowded upbringing in rural England, rural France has a totally different meaning, believe me.

Even in this great modern age rural France definitely remains rural. Everyone knows, or is related to, the rest of the village.

They celebrate together, grieve together, bring their children up together and help each other out.

When the neighbours pig gets slaughtered, everyone comes round to taste the black pudding, the pâté and drink copious amounts house wine.

Talking of pigs, I still order a whole beast from my neighbours in the Loire where I bought my first property, the old village Bakery, with an enormous domed fire fed bread oven in what was to become my main living space.

One arrived just the other day (that would be a pig) so when I start on the preserving of the pâté, black pudding and cured hams, you can guarantee the old guard of retired blue overalls, wine toting elders will be round to offer their professional opinions of how I should proceed and the more wine they help themselves to the more advice I will receive.

Well, actually, I like to set myself a bit of a challenge, simply because I have travelled and I have tasted other versions of similar dishes in other countries using the same cuts of meat or fish, but with ingredients local to them. I can't help my curious mind from mixing it up!

I do cook traditional dishes, of course I do, but I'm also fascinated by foods from all countries. The common denominators being, passion, patriotism, tradition, necessity, availability, quality, and community. All these ingredients make great food and that is why I cook. For all those qualities produce the best results!

Am I making sense so far?

Even better, I get to teach like-minded students from all over the world.

I hope for those of you that have come to me in my Burgundy Cookery School, and for those I teach around the globe, that you will leave at the end with some of the same passion for colour, smell and taste that I found in these markets that inspired me to cook.

For those of you who have yet to experience my style of cooking, and the reasons why I cook, I give you this, my first book.

SHOP. COOK. EAT.

It is a journey into the heart of hidden Burgundy, to my Cookery School, 'La Ferme de la Lochére' where you will be submerged into a Food and Wine extravaganza.

As you leaf through my collection of favourite dishes, I want you to imagine that you are *all* actually here with me! Then you too will be inspired to visit your own local markets, get to know your own local produces, create your own menu plans to make the very best of the seasonal produce that is on your doorstep.

Create a store cupboard, however small, to give you some essential delicious jars bursting with flavours, be inspired to create some fabulous gifts that will impress your friends and family, hold a simple 'al fresco supper', or whip up a last minute picnic lunch to be enjoyed with friends and a good glass of wine!

So, gather your ingredients, put on your aprons because now it's time to get cooking!

A note on 'The French Kitchen'
Cooking for the French is what social media is to teens!

Not a phone, but a kitchen, a place to gather, a necessity, a reason for being, a place to learn, debate, laugh, cry and celebrate.

Having been influenced for many years by French dishes, markets, the people, the wine, it is hardly surprising that my recipes are woven with hints of the traditional with the zing of the modern.

Fresh, fragrant, local and seasonal is the key to inspiring dishes and happy faces.

Contents

SHOP. COOK. EAT.

INFUSION FRUITÉE
BIEN ÊTRE ET PLAISIR
DOUCEUR DE
FRANCE

€ 20

Markets
Welcome to the
market experience

INFUSION FRUITÉE
BIEN ETRE ET PLAISIR
AMARCANDE

INFUSION FRUITÉE
BIEN ETRE ET PLAISIR
NOCTURNE
citron, orange, menthe, anis et
églantier
Moment de détente
à boire chaude ou glacée
6 € 20
100 gr

> "Watch a French housewife as she makes her way slowly along the loaded stalls... searching for the peak of ripeness and flavour. What you are seeing is a true artist at work, patiently assembling all the materials of her craft, just as the painter squeezes oil colours onto his palette ready to create a masterpiece."
>
> *Keith Floyd*

France, as we all know, is famous for its vibrant markets. But, it's not just about the food.

Let's take a Sunday market say in Chalon sur Soane for example, when you have finally beaten your way through the throng of shoppers milling around from stall to stall, and you get to the main square, most of the people will be sitting in the cafés talking at Mac 9, drinking double espresso, wine or Pastis. It's a place to gather and share the week's woes, the highlights and the 'you'll never guess who' gossip that's contagious. The young sit and people watch the other young, the tourists blunder round trying to get a seat on the main terrace whilst the locals shove past and nab the last table.

It's a great place to be. A people watchers paradise!

Each market day has a different type of shopper. I've just given you an example of the weekend market where it isn't just about your weekly shop but more about being seen.

So, at Dijon market on a Tuesday it is mostly a child free serious shopping zone for the pro's, and by pro's I mean the life-long market shoppers who would rather pay that bit more to be sold the best quality of meat for the week, the freshest of fish caught and delivered that morning. They bring their milk bottles and yoghurt pots back to be refilled, pick up the order of promised bones for the dog, and to chat to the sellers whom they have built up a weekly friendship with.

They know exactly what they want and where the best stuff is. I always advise my students to look for the throng of locals around the cheese counter if you just don't know which has the best artichokes, checkout the three deep row of bodies waving their hands in the air demanding attention.

But just beware of shopping trolleys, baskets and sharp elbows that come in just under the ribs if you have unwittingly jumped the queue or heaven forbid started another one!
Mon Dieu!

At the Friday market, pace picks up and the clientele has a distinctly different feel about them. They are in more of a rush, on their way to somewhere else as they head to or

SHOP. COOK. EAT.

from the office; professionals looking for delicious ingredients to treat themselves to at the weekend. The Tuesday shoppers popping back in a fluster as the grandchildren have suddenly decided to visit and they need to impress with a delicious patisserie and succulent joint.

How do I know all this? Well, because I love to wander! To watch and absorb the markets, and the lives and life that makes them tick.

When I take my students into Dijon market, which is an impressive building in its own right, designed by Gustav Eiffel, it can be daunting and knowing where and why you should purchase your tomatoes from that stall down the end or at the stall on the outside is by watching how the other local shoppers make that choice.

Here's a tip! Never buy the first thing you see. Take the time to walk around the whole market, make a point of remembering where it's busy, look out for labels on the veggies and fruit that is normally an indication that it has come in from out of town.

Look at the trader's hands –Why? Because, for example, if you cut fresh asparagus it is normally done with a very sharp long knife which causes the cut to be slanted, they will also still have mud on them and it stains your hand to an orangey brown. Wholesale ones are clean with a straight cut on the stall, tied with an elastic band. Mushrooms can also stain the hands orange, brown or a reddish colour. Veggies with mud on are good; it indicates they have been freshly dug mis-shapened tomatoes and curly cucumbers have not been grown under glass, they are natures true harvest. Different shaped eggs is a good sign that they are free range - my Father's wife has an uncanny knack of always buying boxes of double yokes from the egg man in Chalon market, now that is magic, and very tasty too.

Cheese, fresh, part dried, mouldy, solid how do you choose.

If you can communicate, then ask the cheese lady she will be able to tell you. But rule of thumb, if it's really white and looks soft it will be fresh, the more mature they are the darker the colour and they become slightly smaller as they dry out.

> *"How can you govern a country which has 246 varieties of cheese?"*
>
> *Charles de Gaulle*

In Dijon I hold court with my students and a very jolly cheese producer who is just delightful, enthusiastic and willing to put on an impressive tasting. She even beats the locals off when they elbow in for a freebie, very amusing. Her cheeses are from all over Burgundy and are well worth buying to take back home as she can vacuum pack them. A canny lady indeed.

Not all markets are as impressive as the ones I have just described and it can be disappointing that your own local markets don't offer as much choice. However, before we move on I'll take you to a market just around the corner from me in Semur en Auxois, a medieval small town set on top of pink granite rock with cobbled streets and soaring stone towers.

When I first went there on a Sunday morning, I was so disappointed to see just five or so stalls, with not much left on them.

I think I was a little late and on returning a few weeks later, although up to maybe 10 stalls, they were heaving with super local produce. Cheeses literally from the next village from mine, a snail trader with lots of different jars of prepared snails and even some snail face cream. No, I am not going to expand on that story, you'll have to hear the full-length version when you come visit. Local Charolais beef, rich and tender, homemade jams, honey and honey wines, organic breads and the craziest selection of veggies, totally home grown and definitely not treated with industrial anything.

So you see, if you seek you will find, whether it's an impressive city with a majestic market square or a micro market that actually has all you need for the perfect Sunday lunch or an 'al fresco supper'.

Delicious bites from the market

On a rustic platter arrange a selection of the following bought from a specialist deli. Chorizo saucisson-sliced as thinly as possible. Different types of saucisson-sliced as thinly as possible.

Oils and Vinegars
In small shallow dishes pour organic olive oil, then add 1 tsp of truffle oil. In another small shallow dish pour in fig vinegar. Cut small cubes of foccacia and warm in the oven, use to dip first in the oil then in the fig vinegar – so simple, simply divine!

Foccacia
Roughly torn apart fresh local goats cheese drizzled with olive oil and fig vinegar, decorated with sun blushed tomatoes & basil, gently warmed in the oven for 5mins.

Olives in olive oil and garlic
Marinade a mixture of green and black pitted olives in lemon oil, crushed smoked garlic, herbs de province, a pinch of dried red chilli seeds and black pepper.

Fresh goats cheese with chives, chill, crushed red baie, smashed garlic, crushed black pepper and olive oil
Generously smother a fresh goats cheese with all of the above and enjoy! it's delicious.

Served with delicious chilled rosé or sparkling crémant!

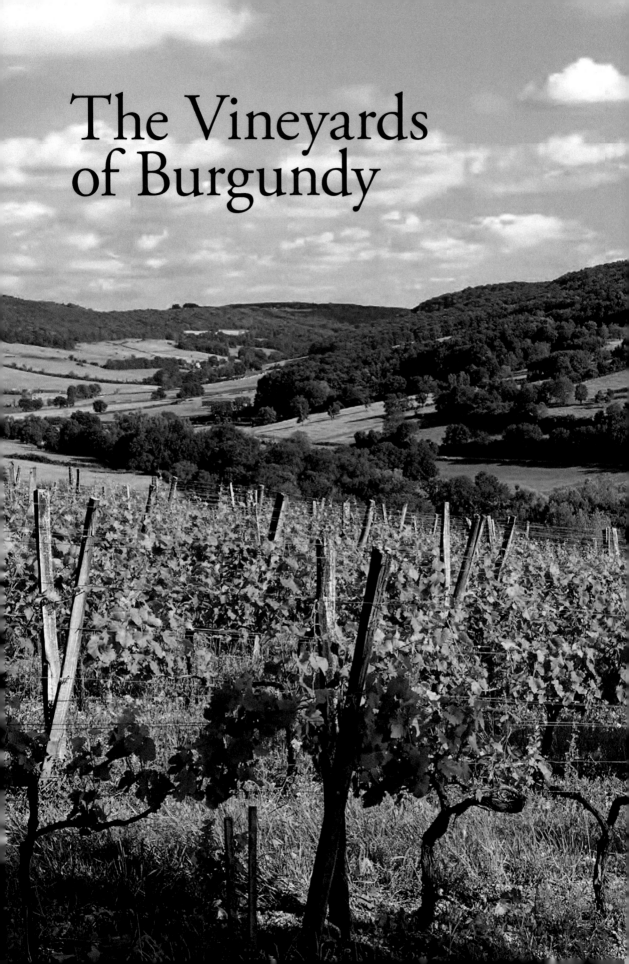

The Vineyards
of Burgundy

> *"A bottle of wine contains more philosophy than all the books in the world."*
>
> *Louis Pasteur*

I could of course sweepingly generalize about the all the wines of France, but I am not going to do it such a disservice. I will concentrate on Burgundy, after all it is what I drink in large volumes throughout the year with my closet vineyards a mere 10 minute drive away, but I'll come to that little gem in a moment.

Most travellers will have heard of the global brand that is 'Burgundy' one might assume that there is little else to know, but you'd be very wrong indeed.

To discover the somewhat complex system of Burgundy wines a visit to the ancient former capital of Burgundy, Beaune, is essential. This medieval town is full of quaint boutique shops, elegant houses, copious Bistro's, fine dining restaurants and traditional cafés as well as a heaving Saturday market and the majestic 'Hospice de Beaune' where the infamous Wine Auction - run by Christie's the Auctioneers, (still held on the 3rd weekend of November, although now rehoused to the undercover market due to it's popularity) and it is the perfect place to set out on a day of discovery through a slither of one of the most famous places in France.

The Côte d'Or, literally translated as the golden coast, although there is no chance of sea, it is actually a limestone and clay soil created millions of years ago as the glaciers flowed down from the Massif Centrale. The side that we are interested in is bathed in sunshine, with perfect drainage thanks to the limestone, which are the ideal conditions for growing Pinot Noir and Chardonnay grapes.

This slender stretch of land meanders either side of Beaune with the Cote de Nuits one side and the Cote de Beaune the other. After chilly frosty winters just laying dormant, gathering strength for the coming Spring the stumpy twisted vines start to awaken and stretch out as if by magic with a good few days of warm sun.

This is the perfect time to get your first glimpse of these beloved and precious vines.

I am extremely fortunate, along with my students, to explore this area with one of the best wine experts in Burgundy. The infamous Brendan Moore. Who is the source of all my knowledge, as I am certainly no oenologist!

But, I do know that it all started with the Monks and their need to produce wine for mass, and it was also safer than drinking the water - good call!

Many of the monks were from aristocratic families, extremely well educated and completely devoted to serving The Lord.

It was in fact them that created the vineyard maps still in use today. They chose the best grape variety for the growing conditions and soon earned an admiral reputation for producing fabulous wines consumed at 'mass'.

Obviously with their reputation growing they soon turned their knowledge into commercial success, plumping up the coffers and living in legendary monasteries.

Finally, the serfs had had enough of toiling in the dirt and rebelled, in typical French style, ousting the monks and dividing the vineyards up between the villages and it's inhabitants.

Moving along to the present day, what the family owns, stays in the family in this region. Traditionally the vineyards pass down from generation to generation but also multiplies through canny marriages.

Driving through the 'terroir' of the vines, it is amazing at just how many names seem so familiar. Due to the labelling of these wines, it will be marked with the name of the village, the name of the producer and the actual name of the strip of land it was grown in and if it's an old vine that goes on there too. It's quite remarkable and makes serving these wines an honor. It almost feels like the producer is sitting and enjoying it with you. Which of course, when my guests at the Cookery School 'La Ferme de la Lochére' get to experience first hand.

Chablis, to the North of Burgundy, is another famous wine growing area. It is slightly disheartening to hear the uneducated using Chablis as the generic name for Chardonnay.

A visit to Chablis on Sunday is a perfect combination of strolling through the vibrant and truly bustling market choosing ingredients for a picnic, then heading off wine tasting in the limestone vineyards, followed by a well deserved break nestling amongst the butterflies in the meadows overlooking the rolling vines.

Close to my heart is the Vignoble of Flavigny, where the film Chocolat was filmed. An enthusiastic, energetic team of dedicated wine growers have bought this not so long ago non existent plot of land to life as it nestles on the hillside looking over to the Monastery still perched on the cliff of this Medieval walled village.

In the mid 19th century the veracious blight know as phylloxera, swept through France killing all the vines. It is in fact an aphid and eventually thanks to American grafted vines the wine makers could start to replant, but not in the area between Chablis, the cote de Nuit and cote de Beaune.

So the fact that these courageous pioneers have actually replanted in my local area deserves admiration and support. Now celebrating their 20th year, it produces good honest wines that are reasonably priced and good to drink now. Sadly they can never attain the coveted AC - Appellation Controle of 1er Cru or Grand Cru, due to the Monks 400 years ago designating the high quality plots still upheld today which cannot be modified. Personally I think that's a trifle unfair, but obviously, I am a lone voice.

I love this place and we are always made to feel welcome, testing the newest blends of wine that aren't even bottled yet, stroll and picnic in the vineyards and are left to explore the grounds and woodlands around the estate.

Planning
The Bones to Perfection

> *"Cooking is an art and patience a virtue... Careful shopping, fresh ingredients and an unhurried approach are nearly all you need."*
>
> *Keith Floyd*

I'm going try and keep this brief as I'm sure you must have noticed by now I like to chatter, but this is the serious stuff, so I'll keep it simple.

If you want to enjoy your guests, spend time with the kids, go dancing, sit on the porch and drink gin then here's what you have to do…get organized and plan well.

Told you it was simple…but here's the rub…it can take a little practice.

Many moons ago, when I was still at school in one of my very first home economic classes (cookery to the layman) we were given a challenge to create a 2 course lunch or dinner.

Not only that but we also had to provide an order of work, shopping list in categories and why we had chosen the dishes as the choices where imaginary people with special dietary requirements.

It was the best thing I ever learned, and if I were asked what tip I would give as the secret to being a successful cook it would be in the planning.

I still sit, plan and write lists. I also do it systematically whilst I'm washing up, driving (I don't think that's been banned yet), walking the dog - like most busy people. It's not rocket science, but when faced with a cooking challenge it can turn the best organized person into a bit of a spin.

When I have a group in the Burgundy Cookery School it is an important skill I know my students appreciate. It really does make cooking so much easier and they all achieve so much more once they've made a plan!

Most people get a recipe and start to cook without actually reading the method properly or even checking they have the correct ingredients.

So firstly work out your menu, the weekly family menu, picnic, friends to supper menu, Christmas, Easter, Birthday, what ever, don't choose an important meal to start trying out a Heston and cook the lamb leg in your teens football sock in the dishwasher unless you've done it before (which hopefully you won't have).

Keep it simple, and do something you're good at or practice ahead of time.

Draw up a shopping list by going through your recipes. As I shop in the market wherever possible, I write mine with the heading of the stall so I keep it easy, organized and saves time – dairy, meat, herbs, veg, bread etc.

Pick up any dry ingredients at a store on the way home then you're ready to start.

Preparing several dishes at once is not as alarming as you might think. Reading the recipes through several times will help to make it clearer, it will become apparent with practice that the more you get done before hand the more relaxed you'll be as the dinning time approaches.

I always aim to be finished an hour before I need, to leave some room for the things that might not go quite accordingly to plan and to go get changed and become the smiley hostess.

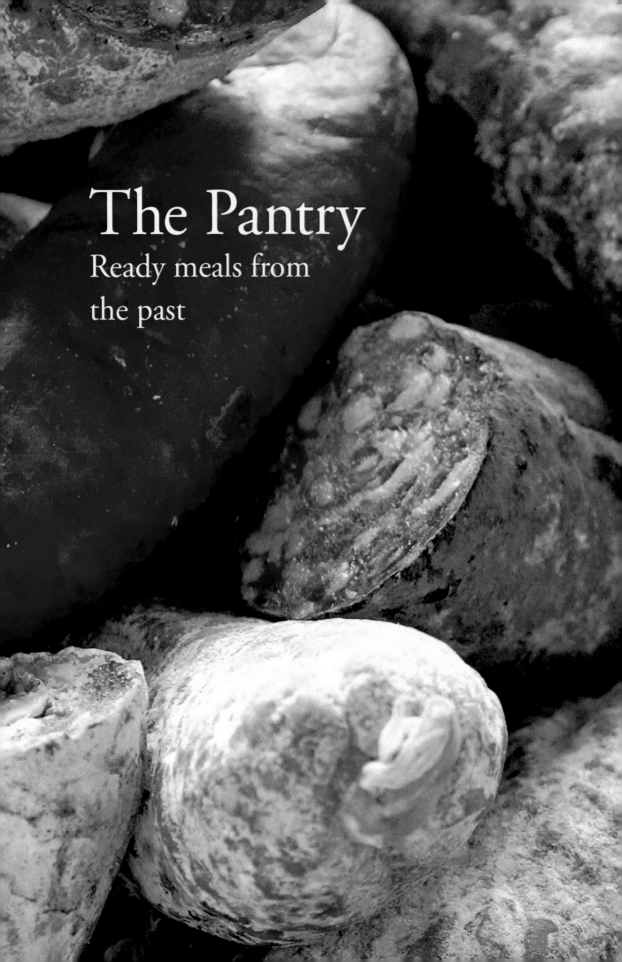

The Pantry
Ready meals from the past

> *"A place
> for everything,
> and everything
> in its place"*
>
> *Isabella Beeton*

In every house I have ever been fortunate enough to live in there has been a pantry, cellar or cool room that I have used for storing food. My Grandmother had a pantry, my Mother a larder. The same thing I guess, except my Mother's was under the stairs. Both had airbricks that allowed ventilation to keep the food cool.

My own cellar in Burgundy runs underneath the entire house. It is divided into four separate rooms. The two smallest were used as pigsty's in the past. I must settle your dismay if you think the French used to keep their pigs in a cellar – they didn't, I promise.

Le Four a Pain, which is at least 400 years old, whose origins were once linked to the 12th Century moated Château just across the Roman bridge from us, doesn't have an under ground cellar but one on ground floor level with the house on the first floor. So, take a breath, it's all perfectly pig friendly here.

Only, I don't have pigs any more. I leave that to my neighbour. My pigsties have been transformed into one large room that is racked out on one side with the wine and the other with bottles, jars, hooks for hams, saucisson and freezers.

In the age of the microwave and instant ready meals from the supermarkets, it is a fascinating way to bring nature and the seasons back into your own kitchen.

As with most vegetable gardens and orchards, when you get it right, and the sun is kind, the garden turns into the magic porridge pot and just keeps growing and growing and growing.

If there was ever any doubt that those cute 45 little tomato plants you put in the ground back in April might not give enough juicy fruit to make you ketchup, you might be eating more than your words as they just keep on appearing day after day. Now you have enough tomatoes to make two years worth of ketchup, over 20 bottles of Passata, stuffed, chopped, chutney, salsa, soup, bloody Mary's. Can you tell I'm speaking from experience?

If this has ever happened to you, you will also know that the same harvest will be reaped from all your neighbours, family and friends. What better thing to take as a gift when you go and stay but a fabulous crate of fresh fleshy tomatoes for

stuffing. Good if you are taking the crate, bad if you are on the receiving end, but it is the thought that counts!

Bottling/canning and freezing is the perfect way to preserve a copious harvest and those crates of gifted produce that have been thoughtfully offered.

It's great fun, very satisfying and imagine, you don't have to go out to the store to pick up ketchup, BBQ sauce, jelly, pâté, you have some pretty gifts to offer at Christmas and when unexpected guests pop in you have ready-made pasta sauces, pesto's and soup already to go. The thing with preserving, bottling/canning and freezing is to not get overwhelmed with the task in hand.

In order to actually produce enough ketchup for two years, prepare bottles of fruit vinegars, red pepper and tomato chutneys, lavender vodka, blackcurrant gin, redcurrant jelly, fruit cheese, elderflower cordials and ginger beer to name but a few, you must plan well and set aside a few days just to make and store.

By planning your calendar like you mark down Birthdays and Special occasions, highlight reminders of when things are likely to be ready. Spring for tender vegetables, summer for soft fruits and berries, Autumn/Fall for most other fruits, vegetables and herbs. Pâtés and saucisson I tend to prepare as I'm coming out of winter, mid to late March.

Researching the techniques from the past on preserving methods is also something I recommend as it leads to a better understanding of why and how it works. Salting, curing, smoking, drying and pickling is an ancient art steeped in history.

Sun drying in hot climates and smoke drying in damper climates were amongst the first techniques of preserving food enabling populations of hunters to travel further as the risk of food deteriorating during transport was less.

Salt was a prized commodity that was worth fighting for, especially in Egyptian times as it was used in conjunction with honey and vinegar to mummify and in medieval times for preserving proteins - meat and fish.

Due to being in such rural areas, the French have always used preserving as the main way to keep their produce for the leaner months.

I know I'm always harping back to the pig, but it is a classic example as how single piece of this animal is used. There is never any waste, just what people choose to eat or not!

Although I have huge respect for the traditional preserving recipes and always follow the rules regarding preparation of equipment, hygiene is everything, and timings for sterilization is vital, I do love to break the mould with some funkier recipes. I really enjoy making different Pesto's, Harissa, Curry pastes and spicy BBQ sauces and ketchup as well as the fruit vinegars. Experimenting with delicious ingredients makes it so much more unique.

Don't be put off by thinking it's just an old method no one does anymore and that it is just the rural communities that do this, it doesn't have to be. Even the city dwellers can store some small bottles of flavoured oils, a few jars of pesto, some potted meats and a tub of aromatic salt to enliven a soup or to throw in some dough. It is guaranteed to impress.

Spices

I used to find it immensely irritating when purchasing spice mixes in small sachets that might just flavour one batch of bread, a simple soup or roasting vegetables.

After a trip a few years ago to Goa, it seemed obvious that I should buy lots of spices and blend my own which is exactly what I did and I've been creating ever since. It has also become my signature in many dishes.

You will notice as you cook through the book, there is often a pinch, handful or sprinkling of various different spices.

I have tried to show restraint, as this is a book about the inspiration I have found through the culture, markets and the people of France, but I have allowed myself the indulgence of using spices as the French did colonise many countries that used spices, so I think, although the link is tenuous, it's permitted. I could fill another book just about how passionate I am about using them in recipes. Fortunately, with the Moroccan, Algerian influence I can find many

"Dearly cherished, prized and exotic, inspiring and mythical, impossible to live without"

Scatty Chef

SHOP. COOK. EAT.

fragrant spices in the local market in big hessian bags. In my cooking, spices are as important as salt and pepper. They complete the taste that I am trying to achieve and this is what people have come to recognize in my style of cooking.

The spice recipes in this book are my favourites, and I have them with me wherever I go. If I'm flying to the USA to work I always have some checked in as I know that my clients will challenge their guests to name the flavours in the bread, or soup , pie crust or tagine. When I teach, it's never a precise measurement, more of a generous pinch or handful. I mix them into pastes and use as marinades for roast vegetables or smother over pork belly to flavour the meat.

Using a variety of Indian - classic curry spices ground and made into pastes to flavour rice, Middle Eastern - citrusy, fragrant flavoured spices ground, mixed with lime juice, fresh coriander, sesame blended to create a bursting marinade for lamb and North African - enormous tastes of cumin, turmeric, dried mint, coriander seeds ground and mixed with dried rose petals for a perfumes vegetable tagine with dates and pomegranates huge influences, massive flavours, endless possibilities.

My repertoire is very extensive and yet there are still so many more to seek out and try. The Caribbean is on my spice hit list for the future.

Making your own spice mixes becomes addictive; all you need is a coffee grinder and a really good Indian, Middle Eastern or North African market, or ethnic supermarket.

Obviously the best place is to travel to India, Israel or Morocco, but that is not always possible, so finding great suppliers is a must, although ordering online can be a great alternative.

When I teach or work in the UK I always visit a wonderful Indian shop where you can buy 50g bags of spices or big sacks, it's very impressive. I am then lost for days to the outside world as I mix, toast grind and create pastes with all the spices I've purchased.

Researching big events I organize is also vital to achieving the standard I know I need to provide for my clients. If the theme is Lebanese, I'll head to London and the Lebanese quarter which can be a real adventure. It pays to do your research and we appeared on the front cover of a Wedding magazine with the Baklava Wedding cake that I built over 1.5 meters high. I still visit that area whenever I get the chance to gather supplies and to soak up the atmosphere, admire the spices bags, talk to the shopkeepers, haggle recipes out of them, and discover new ingredients. That is how I mange to create authentic real flavours from these ancient countries. Having a selection of your favourite hand blended spices in the Pantry means guaranteed success for the simplest of recipes and I definitely recommend it, you won't regret it.

Having a selection of your favourite hand blended spices in the Pantry means guaranteed success for the simplest of recipes and I definitely recommend it, you won't regret it.

Pickles, chutneys, pastes and relishes, oils, dressings and vinaigrettes with a few other bits and bobs thrown in
Oded Schwartz is my inspiration for the mere fact that he shared his passion for preserving with mortals like myself in the simplest of terms.

His book, called simply "Preserving" by Dorling Kindersley, is my Bible and I use it always as a reference to see if I can pickle, cure, keep or smoke anything I might come across to lengthen it's life and expand my Pantry.

I never do things by half and, as we have already discussed, if you have tomatoes and redcurrants a go, your neighbours, family and friends, lock keepers, wine producer (no, no grapes) and total strangers will have an abundance too. Never one to turn down a box of ripe raspberries, or some French beans, I'll take in all the waifs and strays. I'll spend the entire day making chutneys, ketchup, jams and flavoured vinegars. After that I'm set for probably two years.

The thing is, if you say no and the next Spring there is a late frost just as the fruit trees come into flower there will be no fruit that year, so best make hay whilst the sun shines.

My Pantry is a reflection of the seasons, it fills me with great pleasure every time I go and seek out a jar of something from last summer.

> "Experience the pleasure and immense satisfaction of preserving your own food"
>
> *Oded Schwartz*

Dr. Rowland's ultimate bbq sauce and marinade

1 cup vegetable oil
1 cup chopped onions
1 cup tomato ketchup
1 cup Worcestershire sauce
1 cup lemon juice
1 cup sugar

Heat the oil in a large saucepan add the onions and cook gently for 5mins. Add all the other ingredients and bring to a furious boil.

Reduce the heat and simmer for 1hr or until the mixture starts to thicken. Bottle and keep for up to a year.

To keep longer heat seal and it will keep for up to 2 years.

To be used as a relish, marinade, sauce for all meats, bbq's and for a finer sauce for dinner parties use homemade tomato sauce instead of ketchup and sieve before serving over pork belly or other meats.

Watermelon chutney

600g water melon, peeled
  and cubed
200g apple juice
juice and zest of 1½ lemons
300g sugar

Put all the ingredients in a saucepan and cook until the watermelon has become translucent with the sauce slightly sticky, approx. 45-60mins.

Spoon into sterilized jars and seal. Will keep for 6 months. This chutney can be heat sealed for 30mins to prolong its self life for 2 years.

Delicious with smoked salmon, smoked duck or cured ham

Papaya and mango salsa

2 ripe mangos, peeled
  and diced
2 ripe papaya, deseeded,
  peeled and diced
1 sweet red pepper, diced
2 hot red chillis, finely
  chopped
juice and zest of 2 limes
½ grated nutmeg
2tbsp lemon balm, chopped

Mix all ingredients together.

Keep in a Kilner jar and chill until needed.

Will only keep 2 weeks in the fridge.

Tomato ketchup

2kg tomatoes, quartered
500g shallots peeled and
  roughly chopped
75g fresh ginger, peeled
  and grated
6 garlic cloves, peeled and
  smashed
3-4 fresh chilli's deseeded
  and roughly chopped
6 celery stalks, trimmed and
  roughly chopped

for the spice bag
2tbsp coriander seeds
1tsp cloves
1tsp blade mace
tie all the spices into
  a bag using muslin

for every litre of pulp
250ml cider vinegar
75g soft brown sugar
2tsp salt
1tbsp sweet paprika

In a large pan add all the principal ingredients up to and including the spice bag.

Cook for 45mins until the tomatoes have released all their juices.

Remove from the heat, mash the tomatoes using a moulé which will separate the seeds and skin from the juice and pulp. Or use a food processor and then sieve the skin and seeds out.

Return to a clean pan and return the spice bag.

Add the remaining ingredients and cook until the ketchup starts to thicken over a low gentle heat. This could take up to 2 hours.

Stir regularly so that it does not stick on the bottom.

The ketchup will be darker than commercially produced tomato sauce, so don't worry.

Spoon or pour into clean sterile jars or bottles, seal with lids, corks or wax or heat seal for 30mins to increase the shelf life.

Beetroot and ginger salsa

1kg fresh beetroot, peeled
  and finely diced
1kg sour apples, peeled
  and chopped
3 red onions, peeled and
finely chopped
8cm fresh peeled and
  grated ginger
250g brown sugar
1tsp salt
3tsp mixed spice
125ml red wine vinegar

In a large saucepan add all the ingredients except the apple.

Add the ginger, spices, vinegar and sugar.

Simmer for 1hr.

Add the apples and cook for 15mins.

Spoon into clean sterilized jars and seal.

Can be heat sealed and stored for up to 2 years.

Pear, tomato and chargrilled red pepper salsa

**1kg toms skinned, deseeded
and roughly chopped**
**1kg pears, peeled, cored
and roughly chopped**
**500g chargrilled red
peppers, peeled and diced**
450g onions, chopped
**7 celery stalks, chopped
finely**
**4 fresh chillis, deseeded,
chop finely**
1tbsp yellow mustard seeds
1tbsp sweet paprika
1tbsp fennel or dill seeds
200ml water
1ltr cider vinegar
250g soft light brown sugar
1tbsp sea salt

In a preserving pan or large heavy bottomed saucepan add the pears, toms, onions, celery, chillies, paprika, mustard seeds, fennel or dill seeds and water.

Bring to the boil then reduce the heat until the pears are soft.

Add the sugar, vinegar and salt and simmer for 2hrs until the salsa starts to thicken.

Add the chargrilled red peppers 20mins before the end of cooking. Taste.

Serve with hard cheeses, pâtés, cold meats, grilled fish.

Can be heat sealed and stored for up to 2 years.

TIP
Don't be tempted to replace the cider vinegar with balsamic unless it is white balsamic or the salsa just looks black, which is a shame when it has all those lovely colours in it.

Preserved garlic, green olives and pesto salsa

300g preserved garlic cloves,
cut in half - can be found
at the deli counter
300g fresh green olives
cured with parsley, small
amount of brine and
garlic - can be found at
the deli counter - destone
with a cherry stoner
one quantity freshly made
herb pesto (see p.50)
large handful of fresh
coriander
1 small red chilli, deseeded
and finely chopped
salt and freshly ground
pepper

Mix all the ingredients together.

Serve with warm foccacia or gougere's topped with sour cream or stir through freshly made pasta for a crunchy sauce and sprinkle with grated parmesan or any other hard grated strong cheese.

Maple syrup and bourbon marinade for smoking salmon

300ml bourbon
300ml maple syrup
3tsp dijon mustard
4tbsp light brown sugar
1tsp fresh ground black
pepper

In a saucepan whisk together all the ingredients and heat until the sugar has dissolved.

Cool and use to marinade the salmon over night before smoking.

The glaze can smell strong, especially if you don't like bourbon as I don't. However, don't be put off as the flavour in the salmon is very mild.

Tomato coulis

500g tomatoes, peeled,
deseeded and chopped
1tbsp clear balsamic vinegar
1tbsp olive oil
Salt and pepper to taste

Blend all the ingredients and strain.

SHOP. COOK. EAT.

Mint, coriander, parsley and preserved lemon marinade

100g flat leaf parsley,
   washed and chopped
150g fresh mint leaves,
   washed and chopped
150g fresh coriander,
   washed and chopped
9 cloves garlic
10cm freshly peeled and
   grated ginger
3 red chillies, chopped,
   seeds removed
6 freshly squeezed lemons
6 preserved lemons, roughly
   chopped
200ml soy sauce
200ml olive oil
300ml water
200ml runny honey
100ml tarragon or white
   wine vinegar
2tsp salt
1tsp black ground pepper
1tbsp of Ras el hanout

To finish the sauce
juice of 1 lemon
large splash of cream
handful of freshly chopped
   herbs to decorate

Blend all of the ingredients together.

Pour ⅔ of the sauce over the meat and leave to marinade overnight.

The rest is to keep until serving when the remaining ingredients are mixed together and heated gently before spooning over the meats or to be served on the side in a pretty jug.

Cucumber coulis

1 cucumber, peeled
   deseeded, roughly diced
1 red split chilli, deseeded
   and roughly diced
small bunch fresh dill fronds
small bunch fresh chervil
100ml good quality light
   olive oil
juice of ½ lemon
pinch of salt

Blanch until smooth, strain and store in fridge until required.

It will not keep more than a couple of days.

If the coulis separates, whisk until blended.

Perfect with poached salmon, or salmon tartare.

Herb pesto

**3 garlic clove, peeled
and crushed**

**sea salt and freshly ground
pepper**

**a handful of flat leaf parsley,
basil and coriander or and
other combination you
think might work**

**1 cup grated strong hard
cheese, doesn't have to be
parmesan,** *(yes, I know the
classic pesto recipe is, but
keep it local!)*

**1 cup of pine nuts or
almonds or walnuts, toast
the nuts on a baking tray**

300-350ml olive oil

Blend everything into a paste, seal in small jars.

*Use on pasta, risotto with white truffle shavings or as a
marinade for meats (slow roast pork belly).*

*TIP
You can always spice it up with 5 small red chilli's deseeded
(optional).*

Lemon mayonnaise

**2 egg yolks from free
range chickens**

**1tbsp Dijon mustard
or less if you don't
like too much spice**

zest of 1 large lemon

juice of 2 lemons

good quality olive oil

salt and pepper to taste

Put you eggs, salt and pepper, and mustard in either a large
mixing bowl with a tea towel underneath to stop the bowl
spinning or in a food processor.

Start whisking to combine the ingredients and very slowly
add the oil until it starts to become really thick.

When it is thick stop whisking quite so hard and add the
lemon zest and juice.

Combine until it is smooth, but don't over mix or it may split

Taste and adjust the seasoning.

You can add a spoonful or two of crème fraîche to loosen the
mixture and make it creamer if you wish!

Add some chopped coriander or chervil to change the flavour.

Honey and roast garlic dressing

1 whole garlic
extra virgin olive oil for
   drizzling over garlic
300ml extra virgin olive oil
2tbsp balsamic vinegar
2tbsp runny honey
2tsp smooth Dijon mustard
½tsp paprika
pinch of coarse ground
   sea salt

Roast the garlic in a medium oven wrapped in foil and drizzled in olive oil.

In a blender add all the other ingredients apart from the olive oil.

When the garlic is cool enough to handle pop out the cloves (they should be soft and golden) add to the blender.

Blitz the ingredients until it forms a homogeneous paste and drizzle the olive oil in.

Stop and taste, add more vinegar or a squeeze of lemon if you would like it sharper.

If it is too thick then add a small amount of water and blitz again until the desired consistency is achieved.

Lemon scented dressing

450ml Greek yoghurt
1 lemon juice and zest
a selection of fresh herbs
2tbsp olive oil
1tbsp tarragon wine vinegar
coarse sea salt & freshly
   ground pepper and
   a pinch of sugar

Mix everything up in a food blender and chill until needed.

Miso dressing

5g soy sauce
1 egg yolk (free-range)
100g white miso
50g sesame seed oil
35g Japanese rice vinegar
150g olive oil
150g water
60g smooth Dijon mustard

Mix everything together until well blended, chill until needed.

It will keep really well in the fridge for several weeks.

It will be thicker when it first comes out, but just mix well and add a little water if you prefer it to be runnier.

Delicious on a crunchy green salad, french bean salad, smoked duck or salmon.

Fresh orange dressing

**500ml freshly squeezed
  orange juice**
½tsp paprika or chilli flakes
½tsp ground cumin
4 split cardamom pods
1 stick cinnamon
**1 vanilla pod, split
  and scraped**
1tsp smooth Dijon mustard
3 strips orange peel
6tbsp extra virgin olive oil
1tbsp fresh basil leaves
2tbsp maple syrup
3 star anise

Put everything but the olive oil in a saucepan and reduce down by two-thirds.

When the orange juice resembles a light syrup and has cooled, whisk in the olive oil and add extra basil leaves before serving.

Anchovy dressing

12tbsp olive oil
6tbsp red wine vinegar
1tsp Dijon mustard
**generous grind of fresh
  black pepper**
3 clove garlic, pressed
**8 anchovy fillets, chopped
  fine**

Blitz the whole lot in a food processor and store in a jar in the fridge until needed.

Give it a good shake to loosen it up before pouring over.

TIP
If it is still too thick add a little water and shake, keep adding until it is a pouring consistency.

Herb oils

200g rosemary sprigs
400g flat leaf parsley

Rosemary oil
Blanch the rosemary for 20 seconds in boiling salted water, drain and refresh in iced water. Blanch the parsley for 5 seconds in boiling salted water, drain and refresh in iced water.

Blend with the grape-seed oil until smooth.

Basil oil

500g fresh basil leaves
200ml olive oil
100ml grapeseed oil

Blanched for 10 seconds in boiling salted water, drain and refresh in iced water. Blend with the oils until smooth until smooth.

Chive oil

300g freshly cut chives (no
need to blanch these)
250ml grapeseed oil

Blend with the grape-seed oil until smooth.

Mint and coriander oil

500g mint and or coriander
leaves
½tsp ground cardamom
seeds
250ml grapeseed oil

Blanch the leaves for 10 seconds in boiling salted water, drain
and refresh in iced water.

Blend with the grape-seed oil until smooth.

Fennel oil

200g fennel fonds
200g flat leaf parsley
250ml grapeseed oil

Blanch for 10 seconds in boiling salted water, drain and
refresh in iced water.

Blend with grape-seed oil until smooth.

Wild rocket oil

400g wild rocket
(no blanching necessary)
300ml grapeseed oil
pinch of salt

Blend until completely smooth.

Use the herb oil as soon as possible or they will lose their
colour. Approx. 1-2 weeks.

Fabulous for using drizzled over salads and through pasta.

TIPS
*Most herbs must be blanched very briefly in lots of boiling
heavily salted water to retain their colour and flavour.*

Remove and immediately plunge into iced water.

*Pat dry, cut into pieces with scissors (chopping them can
sometimes bruise the herbs) and blend with oil (unscented oil
as a rule) Use enough oil to cover the herbs by approx. 1cm.*

*If making scented oil with rosemary and thyme, add parsley
to give it the green colour as the other herbs are a sludgy
brown colour.*

*Chill the purée for a day in the fridge as this will intensify
the flavour.*

*Strain through a muslin cloth and store the oil in bottles in the
fridge or they can be frozen.*

Spiced oils

Green masala oil

50g green masala paste
200ml grapeseed oil

Blend the ingredients together and leave to macerate for 24hrs. Strain through a muslin cloth and store in sealed bottles.

Tandoori oil

50g tandoori paste
200ml grapeseed oil

Blend the ingredients together and leave to macerate for 24hrs. Strain through a muslin cloth and store in sealed bottles.

Chilli oil

20 split red chilli
1tsp salt
3tsp black peppercorns

Pack the red chilli's into a jar, add the salt and black peppercorns.

Pour over 1ltr warm grapeseed oil. Leave to infuse for 3 weeks. Strain and bottle.

Garlic oil

20 peeled crushed garlic
2tsp salt
2tsp black peppercorns

Pack the garlic into a jar, add the salt and black peppercorns.

Pour over 1ltr warm grapeseed oil. Leave to infuse for 3 weeks. Strain and bottle.

TIPS
These oils are amazing drizzles over plain rice, used for stir frying scallops and prawns etc.

Use these oils within 6 months.

Moroccan merguez spice mix

¼ cup sweet paprika
2tbsp ground fennel seeds
2tbsp ground cumin
1tbsp ground coriander seeds
2tbsp salt
1tsp ground cinnamon
1tsp cayenne pepper
¾tsp black pepper

Grind all the spices up in a coffee or spice grinder.

Aromatic salt

300g maldon salt
   or flaky sea salt
5tsp cinnamon
5tsp all spice
3tsp turmeric
3tsp ground fenugreek seeds
5tbsp dried mint
8tbsp ground almonds

Blend everything together and store in a jar.

Use for decorating soups, as a rub for meat and poultry, in puréed potatoes, over salad and in vinaigrettes and dressings.

Green masala paste

5tsp fenugreek seeds soaked
   over night so that
   they swell up to a
   jelly like consistency
30 fresh garlic cloves,
   peeled and smashed flat
250g freshly grated ginger
250g fresh mint leaves
250g fresh coriander leaves
500ml white vinegar
10tsp salt
12tsp ground turmeric
8tsp chilli powder, more
   if you like it spicier
3tsp ground cloves
6tsp ground cardamom seeds

Blend all the ingredients to make a paste, store in a jar and top with a small amount of hot oil to form a seal.

Makes approx. 1.5kg.

To cook you will need to heat up 1tbsp vegetable oil and 2tsp sesame oil to every 50g paste, stir until the paste starts to give off it's spicy aroma.

Harissa

2tsp caraway seeds
2tsp coriander seeds
2tsp cumin seeds
10 red chillis, deseed
1 chargrilled red
   pepper, chopped
6 cloves garlic
a few coriander leaves
spoonful lemon juice
80ml olive oil

Toast the spices in a hot pan for 2mins to release the flavour, cool, then grind in electric grinder.

Blend all ingredients together to form a paste with a little oil.

Basic vinaigrette

6tbsp extra virgin olive oil
2tbsp balsamic vinegar
pinch of coarse ground
   sea salt
freshly ground black pepper
1tsp smooth Dijon mustard

Put all ingredients together in a jam jar and give it a good shake.

This can be stored at room temperature in bottles. Herbs, garlic and shallots can all be added to change this basis and versatile vinaigrette. Different vinegars can also replace the balsamic used in this recipe.

Walnut vinaigrette

4tbsp grape seed oil
2tbsp walnut oil
2tbsp white wine vinegar
pinch of coarse ground
   sea salt
Freshly ground black pepper

Put all ingredients together in a jam jar and give it a good shake.

Too much walnut oil will make the vinaigrette too strong.

French vinaigrette 'Yannick's' way

400ml oil *(not olive)*
250ml red wine vinegar
1-2tsp Dijon mustard,
   depending on the strength
   you want
salt and pepper

Mix mustard, oil salt and pepper together then slowly whisk in the vinegar. Don't add all the vinegar at once as it might be too sharp. If you do add too much add a pinch of sugar or add a little white balsamic.

TIPS
You can store it in a jam jar for ages in the fridge.

You can add a little walnut vinegar if you wanted to add a little extra taste or maybe some raspberry vinegar.

Adding ½ a crushed clove of garlic is also really tasty, but don't add too much.

Fruit vinegars

2kg of fresh fruits such as raspberries, strawberries, redcurrants, blackcurrants, blackberries
1.5ltrs cider vinegar
granulated sugar

In a large bowl gently crush the fruits with a potato masher to extract the juices. Pour over the vinegar, cover with a clean cloth or a tight fitting lid and leave to soak for 5 days in a cool dark place.

Drain the juice into another large bowl through a jelly bag. This can take all day, but you can gently give the bag a squeeze from time to time. For every litre of juice add 800g sugar. Dissolve the sugar in the juice over a low heat. Once the sugar has dissolved turn up the heat and bring the juice to a boil for 15mins. Remove any impurities with a spoon that are floating on the top of the juice.

Cool slightly and store in sterilized bottles. Seal when cold and store in a dark cool place for up to and slightly beyond 1 year.

These are beautiful gifts if stored in pretty bottles.

Fig and honey vinegar

600g soft dried figs, roughly chopped
2ltrs white wine or tarragon vinegar
200ml runny local honey
5tsp fresh thyme leaves
3tsp slightly crushed white pepper corns
2 star anise
1 small stick of cassia bark

Mix all ingredients in a large bowl and put in your storage vessel of choice. Leave for 1 week in a cool dark place.

Sieve the liquid and pour into sterilized bottles. Label and keep in a cool dark place.

One large sterilized plastic tub or sterilized glass jar. Pretty bottles to store with tightly closing lids or corks.

This vinegar will keep for at least a year if not longer.

Bread and pastries

> "Good bread is the most fundamentally satisfying of all foods and good bread with fresh butter, the greatest of feasts."
>
> *James Beard*

The process of making bread for me is therapeutic.

Not only that it's one of the most important jobs for a busy Chef, amateur or professional. So many recipes call for both sweet and savoury doughs and pastry, industrially made ones will rarely give you the result you want. The satisfaction of making these fundamental kitchen essentials is enormous and I implore you to give it a go.

The time it takes to actually make is minimal and I fail to grasp exactly why anyone would buy a bread machine apart from the obvious convenience of the whole thing. But, that's missing the point of making your own bread! It's about the journey, what you choose to use as flour, if you add olive oil for a savoury rustic loaf to have with soup or a spoon of honey and grains for breakfast toast. It's so easy to do and takes very little time.

You just have to be around the kitchen or close by after a couple of hours to knock it back and then rise again.

Make 4 times the recipe and freeze 3 of the loaves; it works really well and great to have on hand.

At Christmas I always make brioche. I start the dough the night before, let it rise as I'm finishing up with last minute preparations for a stress free Christmas Day, knock it back pop in the fridge, take it out in the morning, shape and leave to rise as the coffee goes through, bake and voilà, fresh buttery brioche ready to be smothered with raspberry jam. So simple, so good!

Quick easy focaccia is a great option for lunch or picnic. It doesn't need to rise as much as bread and whilst it's proving, fry off some ratatouille style vegetables, brush the dough once pushed out into the tin with some pesto from the pantry, spread over the veggies and dot with goats cheese and it's done!

Using bread, or pastry dough, opens up a huge possibility to create a style that you will become known for, just by adding some simple extras into the crust. A sprinkle of chopped dill for a salmon and courgette tart, herbs de province thrown into a crust for quiche Lorraine or caraway seeds for smoked haddock and leek pie.

It couldn't be easier, but have you or anyone you know thought about it before? Not having enough time to make pie crust dough is no excuse in my book - sorry! I'm a busy person to, and no, I'm not perfect, but I'd rather use my pie crust dough than a shop one, so I make them in batches and freeze them, take out to defrost the night before or line pie tins and freeze them until needed. Using foil dishes is a good idea if you're pie dish poor!

Set aside a place in the freezer for pastry and bread, get kneading, it will transform the way you look at the processed stuff!

Basic white bread dough

700g strong white bread flour
2tsp salt
2 sachets easy blend yeast *or* **45g fresh yeast dissolved in 160ml warm milk and a pinch of sugar**
2tbsp extra virgin olive oil *(more for savoury)* **or 25g butter**
450ml warm water
30g runny honey

Mix flour, salt and yeast together in a large bowl, add the water oil/butter.

Turn out onto a clean floured surface and knead well for 15mins or until very smooth.

Return it to the bowl, cover with a tea towel and leave to rise until doubled in size. Turn out and knock back, shape loaves or rolls.

Place in chosen dish and leave to rise a second time. Brush with egg wash and bake in a pre-heated oven 220°C, 425°F for approx. 25-40mins.

Place a small pan of water in the bottom of the oven to create a little steam if you do not have a steam oven. This will create a crusty top!

Turn out and leave to cool.

Herbs, garlic, grated cheese, sun-dried tomatoes, black olives and rosemary, grains & nuts can all be added to this basic recipe to create unique and exciting breads.

Warm aromatic bread

250g white bread flour
250g wholemeal flour
1x 7g pkt easy blend yeast *or* **30g fresh yeast dissolved in 160ml warm milk and a pinch of sugar**
pinch of freshly ground pepper
30g aromatic salt (see spices chapter for recipe)
450ml warm water
1tbsp olive oil
2tsp mixed dried herbs

Mix all the dry ingredients together and slowly pour in the warm water & oil. Turn out and knead until smooth – approx. 10mins.

Place the dough back in the bowl, cover with a tea towel and leave to double in size in a warm place.

Preheat oven to 220°C, 425°F. Knock back and divide into 10 rolls. Place on a non stick baking tray and leave to rise again somewhere warm.

Cook until rolls are golden brown and sound hollow when you tap them upside down. Cool, but keep warm.

Brioche

25g fresh yeast
70ml warm milk
15g salt
500g flour
6 eggs
350g soft butter
30g sugar
1 egg yolk, lightly beaten
  with 1tbsp milk

Place yeast and warm milk in the mixing bowl, stir with a fork and add the salt. Add the flour and eggs and knead with a dough hook until smooth and elastic, approx. 10mins by machine, 20mins by hand.

Beat the butter and sugar together and gradually add to the dough. Continue to mix for 5mins by machine, 15mins by hand. The dough should be smooth and glossy.

Cover the bowl with a clean cloth and leave to rest in a warm place for 2hrs. Knock back the dough briskly in swift flipping motion no more than 3 jests. Cover and leave in fridge for several hours, but no more than 24hrs.

Place dough on lightly floured surface and shape into ball, or balls. Glaze with egg wash and leave to rise for 1½hrs for large brioche 20mins for small.

Preheat oven to 220°C, 425°F. Glaze again and bake for 40-45mins for large, 8-10mins for small.

Rye, spelt and white bread

300g strong white bread
  flour
500g wholemeal spelt flour
300g wholemeal rye flour
2tsp salt
2 sachets easy blend yeast *or*
  45g fresh yeast dissolved
  in 160ml warm milk and
  a pinch of sugar
2tbsp extra virgin olive oil
2tbsp honey
800ml warm water if using
  fresh yeast but up to
  1ltr warm water if
  using easy blend yeast

Mix flour, salt and yeast together in a large bowl if using easy blend yeast. If using fresh yeast, crumble the yeast into a bowl with the salt, sugar and warm milk, whisk briefly and leave to rise for 20mins.

Make a well in the centre and pour in the yeast, water, honey and olive oil. Mix until it forms a firm dough.

Turn out onto a clean floured surface and knead well for 15mins or until very smooth. Return it to the bowl, cover with a tea towel and leave to rise until doubled in size.

Turn out and knock back, shape loaves or rolls. Place in chosen mould and leave to rise a second time.

Bake in a pre-heated oven 220°C, 425°F for approx. 25-40mins. Place a small pan of water in the bottom of the oven to create a little steam if you do not have a steam oven. This will create a crusty top. Turn out and leave to cool.

Pissaladière

1 quantity of basic bread
  mix. *To that add*
2tsp herbs de Provence

for the topping
2 heaped tsp Dijon mustard
2 heaped tsp tapenade
white anchovies or preserved
  classic anchovies
black olives
salt and freshly ground
  black pepper
drizzle olive oil
25g butter
pinch brown sugar
4 large white onions, finely
  sliced
4 cloves garlic crushed
5 juniper berries
2 cloves
glass of white wine
splash of vinegar

Whilst the bread is rising, melt the butter in a large frying pan with the oil.

When it is starting to bubble add the sliced onions, sugar, berries, cloves pepper and salt. When it softens add a splash of vinegar and reduce down, then add a glass of white wine and reduce again. You are trying to achieve a caramelized effect.

In a bowl mix together the black olive tapenade and the Dijon mustard. Roughly roll out your risen dough onto a baking tray, and spread with the mustard mix.

Preheat oven to 180°C, 350°F. Spread the onion mixture over the dough that and decorate with the anchovies in a lattice design. Place black olives in the squares.

Sprinkle over some herbs de Provence and a drizzle of olive oil and bake until well risen and the bread is golden brown.

Blini's

500g 50/50 plain white
  and wholemeal or
  buckwheat flour
1 sachet of easy blend yeast
3 eggs, separated
500ml warm milk
½tsp salt
a little oil for cooking

In a large bowl mix together the dry ingredients, crack in the egg yolks and slowly whisk in the warm milk. Cover and set aside for at least an hour.

Whisk up the egg whites until frothy and gently fold into the delicate blini mixture. Heat up a large heavy bottomed pan and brush with a little melted butter or oil.

Take a dessert spoon and carefully drop into the frying pan to form a small round disc. Do this all round the pan leaving room for them to spread just a little. Leave them for approx. 1min then gently flip over to cook the other side.

Take out and cool on a cooling rack.

Use as canapés or freeze on trays, pop into bags and use when needed.

Pasta dough

250g plain flour
7 egg yolks + 1 extra egg
splash of olive oil
splash of water
pinch of lemon salt

Pile the flour onto a work top and make a well in the middle big enough to hold the rest of the ingredients.

Break in the eggs, add the salt, water and olive oil and start to draw the flour in until you have a dough that feels moist but that does not stick to your fingers – leave to rest for a few minutes, then knead until smooth for approx. 15mins.

Don't overwork the dough or it will become dry. Wrap well and chill for an hour.

Roll out using a pasta machine and use for whatever purpose you have intended.

Hot water pastry

1kg flour
400ml water
240g butter
140g lard
2 level tsps salt

Sieve the flour and salt together. Rub in the butter.

Melt the lard and water together and bring to a frothy simmer. Take off the heat and pour into the flour and butter. Mix to form a smooth dough. Be careful not to burn your hands, it's super hot.

Cover and leave to rest for 30mins. Turn out onto a floured surface and flatten to form a triangle. Fold the dough as for puff pastry - into thirds. Repeat and leave to rest again for 30mins. The dough is ready to use.

I love using this dough, it's like massaging a warm body! It also creates fantastically crunchy pastry. Brilliant for pork pies and sausage rolls!

Real puff pastry

1kg flour
3tsp salt
100g soft butter
400ml water
800g chilled butter
50ml white wine vinegar

Sieve the flour onto a clean dry worktop. Add the melted butter, salt, vinegar and water.

Mix with your fingertips and then gradually bring in the flour to form a firm ball of dough, but be careful not to overwork. Wrap and chill for several hours.

Remove and unwrap the dough and roll out on a lightly floured surface. Using the rolling pin, roll out 4 corners (like ears!) with a mound left in the middle. Bash the chilled butter with the rolling pin on the worktop, and place in the centre of the dough on the mound. Cover with a corner until the butter is covered all the way round and now forms a square. Chill for 30mins.

Remove and unwrap. Roll out on a floured surface into a rectangle. Fold into thirds as before, turn and repeat, chill. Repeat twice more resting for 30mins between every 2 turns.

TIP
I make mine once a week when I'm on a roll, just a habit left over from a hotel I used to work in. Keep it wrapped up and use when needed. If keeping for a few days then only do 4 turns and do the last 2 on the day you use it!

Easy puff pastry

1kg flour
1kg room temperature butter, diced into small cubes
3tsp salt
½ltr iced water

Sieve the flour onto a clean dry worktop. Make a well in the middle and add the butter and salt. Mix the butter and salt together in the flour circle to form a lumpy paste.

Gradually add the iced water. Don't over mix and do not knead. Roll out the dough into a rectangle and fold into thirds, top to middle bottom to middle, turn and repeat, wrap and chill. Repeat twice more. Chill for the last time and then use as normal.

This is a really quick way to make puff pastry, but be aware that it doesn't keep for a long as puff pastry and it will not rise as much!

Basic shortcrust pastry

300g plain flour
185g butter
1 free range egg
1tsp coarse ground sea salt
a dash of milk

In a food processor add all the ingredients apart from the egg and the milk. Blitz for a few moments until it forms fine breadcrumbs. Add the egg and a splash of milk. Pulse the mixture until it forms a ball.

Turn out onto a floured surface, roll into a ball, wrap in clingfilm and chill in the fridge for 45mins. You can freeze it at this stage.

TIP
I use this as the basis for all my quiches but always add 2tsp of fresh mixed herbs or just one herb to give it extra flavour. Making a large batch and freezing them in balls means you always have a supply to make a quick and easy quiche or pie.

Sweet shortcrust pastry two ways

300g plain flour
200g butter
125g icing sugar
3 egg yolks
zest of one lemon or a small
    tsp of vanilla essence
pinch of salt

or
300g flour
50g ground almonds
180g butter
125g icing sugar
1 egg and another yolk
pinch of salt
zest of one lemon or a small
    spoon of vanilla essence

In a food processor add all the ingredients apart from the egg. Blitz for a few moments until it forms fine breadcrumbs. Add the eggs and pulse the mixture until it forms a ball.

Turn out onto a floured surface, roll into a ball, wrap in cling film and chill for 1hr.

You can freeze it at this stage.

Choux pastry

150ml water
150ml milk
120g chilled diced butter
5g salt
190g plain flour
4 large free range eggs or
  5 smaller ones

Preheat the oven to 220°C, 425°F but if you know that your oven is hot make it 10°C lower we all know how temperamental ovens can be!

In a saucepan bring the milk, water salt and butter to a frothy simmer.

Sift the flour onto a sheet of baking parchment and then sift again just to get a bit more air in. When the liquid has boiled take off the heat and pour in the flour. Using a wooden spoon stir the mixture in the saucepan until it has become smooth.

Put the saucepan back on the heat and stir until the paste comes away from the pan – no more than 30sec or so or the mixture will be too dry. Put the paste in a mixing bowl – steady the bowl with a tea towel and roll up your sleeves for the next stage!

Crack the eggs in a bowl and whisk with a fork – not a whisk – you are trying to get big air bubbles in the mixture like an omelette not small bubbles as for a sponge cake. Gradually add the egg to the paste beating well in-between times. You are trying to incorporate as much air as possible – when you are making a cake by hand you tend to beat round and round the bowl. This is more of a dig down and lift up motion best achieved I think by holding the bowl at a sharp angle tucked under ones armpit! It gets a little tiring towards the end but the mixture should be smooth and very shiny.

If you are piping the mixture it can be slightly runnier than if you are spooning it out. If you see that the mixture may be becoming too runny stop adding the last egg. Spoon or pipe small blobs on a lined baking sheet. Bake in the pre-heated oven. Cooking time will vary depending on your oven and also the size of the choux puffs that you have made.

After 15-20mins prop the oven door open slightly to let the steam out or they will go flat.

Continue to cook until the choux puffs are dry and light to pick up.

Cheese and smoked bacon muffins

550g plain flour
4tsp baking powder
100g chopped cheddar
  cheese or any other
  strong cheese
200g smoked lardons,
  cooked and cooled
3 free range eggs
pinch of salt
pinch of freshly cracked
black pepper
350ml milk
150g melted butter

In a large bowl, combine all the dry ingredients.

In a another bowl, beat the egg, milk and butter. Gently stir into dry ingredients, but don't stir too long.

Spoon mixture into muffin cases two thirds up and bake for 15-20mins at 200°C, 400°F.

Serve warm with Winter Salad and Ripe Camembert.

Crumble mix with oats

280g plain flour
100g rolled oats
130g sugar
225g chilled butter, diced
  into small cubes

Rub all the ingredients together and keep in the fridge until needed.

Baked crumble mix with brown sugar and pecans

350g flour
150g brown sugar
80g pecan nuts, roughly
  chopped
225g chilled butter dices
pinch of cinnamon

Rub all the ingredients together to form rough crumbs, spread out on a baking sheet and bake for 20mins until it starts to take on a toasted appearance. Stir twice whilst baking.

Take out of oven and cool. Break up into crunchy crumble bits and use with as the topping to a red plum, ginger and lime zest crumble.

Croissant recipe from 'Frederique' my local baker

500g flour
1 egg
10g salt
125g butter, room
   temperature
30g yeast
roughly 200-300ml water
20g sugar

Make a mound out of the flour on the worktop. Using your fingertips make a well in the centre right down so you can see the worktop.

In the base add all the other ingredients except the butter. Slowly mix the ingredients in the well with your fingertips until the salt and sugar have dissolved, then gradually draw in the flour until you have smooth dough. You may need to add extra water several times to achieve this but try not to add any more flour.

With a rolling-pin roll out four ears from the centre of the dough whilst leaving a raised mound in the middle.

Place the butter on top of the mound and taking the 1st dough ear, stretch slightly and fold over the butter. Repeat with the other three ears until you have formed a square.

Lightly flour the dough underneath on the worktop and on top and the rolling pin. Roll out a rectangle approx. 30cm.

Take the top edge and fold by a third then take the bottom edge and fold that by a third to sit on top of the 1st fold. Turn your dough so it looks like you would open a book i.e. left to right.

Roll upwards and down again until you have another 30cm rectangle and repeat the folding process, leaving to rest 10-15mins between each roll. Repeat this four more times – the more times you fold, the more layers in your croissant.

Finally roll out into a thin rectangle approx. 50cm score in half from side to side, then score triangles. You should get 5-6 per length, so 10-12 in total. In the middle of the largest side of the triangle cut a small nick then roll up from that side to form a tube, Curve the end round to form a croissant shape, place on baking tray, glaze with egg wash and leave to rise for 45mins.

Bake in 200°C, 400°F oven for 20-25mins until golden brown.

1 onion, peeled and finely
   chopped
15g butter
200g girolle mushrooms,
   finely chopped (any tasty
   firm mushroom will do,
   not cépes, as they are
   too soft)
3tsp fennel seeds,
2tsp nigella seeds
pinch of salt
½tsp cracked black
   pepper
120g fresh goats cheese
½tsp fresh thyme

To make savoury filling for croissant

In a heavy bottomed skittle, sauté pan melt the butter and soften the onions until transparent. Add the mushrooms, season with salt and pepper. Cook for a further 5mins.

Add the spices and thyme and cook for a further 2mins. Chill. Add the goats cheese/blue cheese or any other type of tasty cheese to the mushrooms and onions.

Divide between the croissants after they have been rolled out, then roll up as you would to create a chunky delicious croissant.

Soups
and stocks

"Smooth and silky, coarse and hard core soup, it is what it is simply delicious!"

The Scatty Chef

You will not be surprised to hear that the secret to a good sauce, or soup, is the quality of the stock. It's in most of the cook books that you will ever buy, the shortcut shop bought version will never give you the depth of flavour that a home made stock will. Sorry, but that's the truth!

Making stock is not rocket science, it's just bones, veggies herbs and some spices, depending on what stock you're making, gently and slowly cooked to draw all the flavour from the ingredients into the liquid, carefully strained and stored in the fridge or freezer until needed.

For seafood dishes, I prefer crabs and or lobster, as the flavour is milder than using fish. Chicken for me has to be free range, of course, and I always make the stock from the roast chicken we just ate and then it gets stored in the freezer.

My beef stock has to include some oxtail, I just love the flavour it gives after hours of cooking, roasted with other beef or veal bones (rosé veal that sees the light of day not the caged veal that should be avoided at all costs) caramelizing the remaining meat, giving the stock it's colour and flavour.

Vegetable stock is all the best from the garden. I have two slightly different versions. One a little Spring like and the other a stronger earthier sock for Winter vegetable soups and stews.

These basic essential stocks will make so much difference to the finished dishes you will never go back once you've used them.

I said that salads were versatile but what about the humble soup! All over the world people eat soup. From our childhood, there must be one soup you will always remember. It's a classic comfort food, don't you think?

Light delicate broths of wild mushrooms, or Lobster with a hint of lemon ravioli, richer creamy veloute's, maybe of Jerusalem Artichokes or Celeriac with aromatic salts. Thick chunky soups are more of a main course, hearty and filling Moroccan Fish and Chorizo tagine style, Chicken and Minnesota Black Rice Gumbo, Meaty Lamb chunks with cabbage and beans, Vegetable soup with pestou, French Onion soup with garlic cheese toasted wedges, real soup, real food soo good.

French onion soup

100g butter
1tbsp olive oil
1.5kg red onions, thinly
   sliced
10 sprigs fresh thyme, off
   the stalks
5 fresh bay leaves
10 juniper berries, lightly
   crushed
4 whole cloves
3 cloves garlic, crushed with
   the back of a knife
sea salt and freshly ground
   pepper
30g soft brown sugar
2tbsp white wine vinegar
½ bottle french dry white
   wine (more if you like!)
2.5ltrs vegetable or chicken
   stock
8 slices of French bread,
   grilled and covered with
   grated emmental, Comte
   or Beaufort

In a large saucepan, melt the oil and butter and cook the onions gently for 10mins.

Add the thyme, 2tsp sea salt, the pepper and sugar and cook for another 15-20mins until the onions are caramelized and start to stick.

Pour over the vinegar and reduce down until it has been completely absorbed by the onions.

Then add the white wine and reduce by half.

Add the vegetable or chicken stock, bay leaves, garlic and all the other spices.

Simmer slowly for 45mins covered by a tight fitting lid to contain all the steam and intensify the flavour.

Taste and adjust the seasoning.

Before serving the soup, place a slice of toasted French bread, rubbed with a clove of garlic covered with grated cheese in the bottom of each bowl and ladle the hot soup on top.

Petit pois velouté with lemon and mint

2kg petit pois
4 peeled potatoes
bunch of spring onions,
   cleaned and finely
   chopped
2.5ltrs of vegetable stock
   or chicken stock, hot
4 cloves garlic, smoked if
   you can find it
3tbsp fresh mint leaves
1tbsp olive oil
zest of 2 lemons
1tbsp olive oil

In a large saucepan, add the olive oil and sweat the spring onions for 2mins. Add the petit pois, potatoes and garlic, cook for a further 3mins then add the stock and the mint leaves and lemon zest. Cook for 15mins until the potatoes are tender.

Take off the heat and mix with a blender until smooth. Return to the saucepan and adjust the seasoning.

Pour piping hot into your dishes and decorate with a sprinkling of spice mix and a swirl of cream and rocket oil.

Céleri-rave velouté with aromatic spice, coconut milk and tarragon scones

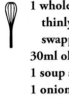

1 whole celeriac, peeled, and
   thinly sliced. Can be
   swapped for pumpkin
30ml olive oil
1 soup spoon aromatic spice
1 onion, peeled and finely
   chopped
1 glass of white wine
1.5ltrs vegetable stock
1 tin coconut milk
sprigs of fresh tarragon or
   other green herb
fresh sea salt & black pepper

In a large bowl pour in ½ the oil and aromatic spices.

Add the celeriac and using your hands toss in the oil and
spices until well covered. Heat the remaining oil in a large
heavy bottomed saucepan.

Add the onion and soften without colouring, then add the
celeriac and mix well.

Add the white wine and vegetable stock. Season with pepper
and a pinch of salt. Cover with a greaseproof paper lid, and
the lid of the saucepan, simmer for 20mins.

Puree the celeriac, adding most of the coconut milk to the
soup. Warm through and serve into warm bowls.

Decorate with a swirl of cream or rocket oil, a sprig or two
of chervil and a sprinkling of aromatic spice.

Serve with some delicious warm tarragon scones.

Tarragon scones
Preheat oven to 230°C.

300g self raising flour
½tsp salt
1tsp baking powder
4tsp chopped fresh tarragon
60g butter or margarine
165ml milk

Sieve the dry ingredients, add the herbs, rub in the
margarine, and then stir in the milk.

Knead and roll out gently to 2.5cm.

Cut out 12 circles and cook for approx. 10mins when they
are risen and golden.

Velouté of topinambour (Jerusalem artichokes)

1kg peeled fresh
   topinambour, roughly
   chopped - (Jerusalem
   artichoke) *I just had to
   put the French name in, it
   sounds so great when you
   try and pronounce it!*
2ltrs fresh chicken or
   vegetable stock
knob of butter
2 onions peeled and roughly
   chopped
juice of 1 lemon
1 sprig of fresh tarragon
200ml white wine
600ml cream
Salt and freshly ground
   black pepper

Melt the butter in a large pan, then soften the onions gently for 5-10mins.

Throw in the topinambour (Jerusalem artichokes), tarragon and lemon juice.

Stir and sweat for 5mins trying not to colour.

Add the white wine and continue to cook until the wine has reduced by half.

Add the stock and cook until the topinambour is soft. Blend until really smooth and then add the cream.

If the velouté is slightly thick just add a little boiling water to thin.

Pour into bowl piping hot, swirl a splash of rocket oil on the top, then one of olive oil and scatter some aromatic salt on top – you can also add a small spoon of chilli pesto for an extra kick!

Lobster broth

50ml vegetable oil
4 lobster bodies, roughly
   chopped to fit into
   your pan
400g chopped tomatoes
300g chopped carrots
1.5ltrs vegetable stock
generous bunch of tarragon
600ml double cream

Heat the oil in a large pan and add the lobster shells. Cook until they are red then add the tomatoes, tarragon and carrots. Cook for over a gently heat for approx. 1hr 30mins, skimming off impurities every now and then.

Strain the stock and then crush the bodies with a rolling pin to extract even more juice. Strain into a clean pan and reduce down by half.

Add the cream and bring to a gentle simmer, reducing down again. Taste and adjust the seasoning. Before serving whisk up until it becomes frothy.

Carrot and pumpkin soup

2kg carrots, peeled and roughly chopped
¼ medium sized pumpkin, cut in half, deseeded, peeled and roughly chopped or you can use butternut squash instead
4 cloves garlic, peeled and smashed with the back of a heavy knife
2 onions, peeled and roughly sliced
handful of fresh marjoram or coriander
1tsp freshly ground coriander seeds
2.5ltr chicken stock (or veg)
sea salt and freshly ground black pepper
1tbsp aromatic salt
knob of butter
splash of olive oil
3 fresh bay leaves

In a large saucepan, melt a knob of butter with a splash of olive oil, and when it is starting to bubble add the onion, carrots and pumpkin, toss in the oil and butter, reduce the heat so that it sweats the vegetables without colouring them - approx. 5mins.

Add the aromatic salt mix, fresh herbs ground coriander seeds, bay leaves, salt and pepper.

Coat all the vegetables and continue to sweat - approx. 3mins.

Add the stock and the garlic.

Cover and simmer until the vegetables are tender when you test with a knife.

Remove the bay leaves and blend the soup until thick and creamy with no lumps.

Add extra stock or water if the soup is too thick.

Serve in heavy bowls with a spoon of crème fraîche in the middle a drizzle of oil, and a slice of crispy bacon and a giant cheese straw.

Not your classic tomato soup

3kg ripe mixed tomatoes
3 large white onions, peeled and sliced
olive oil
3 cloves of garlic, smoked if possible
5cm shredded fresh ginger
3 large bunches of coriander, or basil
1ltr bottled tomato sauce from the garden if possible
1 small fresh red pepper
big spoon brown sugar
8 anchovies
1 block coconut cream paste

Roast the tomatoes and red pepper in a hot oven with a good splash of olive oil, onions, salt and freshly ground black pepper until they start to colour round the edges approx. 40mins.

In a separate pan heat up a knob of butter, cook quickly the fresh coriander, ginger, chilli and garlic. Add the coconut paste, onions and tomatoes, anchovies and season.

Blend until smooth. Taste and adjust the seasoning if necessary.

Serve piping hot with some delicious pan fried pancetta strips or pan fried scallops.

SHOP. COOK. EAT.

Monkfish, chorizo and butternut squash autumn curry tagine soup

1.5kg fresh monkfish

1kg mussels

1 fresh saucisson chorizo, skin off and finely sliced in the diagonal, then cut in half again

1 small butternut squash, peeled, deseeded and chopped into cubes

4 shallots, finely chopped

2 cloves garlic, peeled and crushed

3cm fresh ginger, peeled and grated

2 red chillis, deseeded and finely chopped

2tsp ground turmeric or a piece of fresh turmeric, peeled and grated

2tsp ground coriander

2 tins coconut milk approx. 800ml

300ml fish stock

zest and juice of 2 limes

a handful of chopped coriander or pineapple sage to serve

Fry the shallots until soft.

Throw in the chorizo, cook until the juice oozes out of the chorizo and gently remove from the pan – set aside.

In a large bowl toss the butternut squash in a splash of olive oil, salt and pepper. Add to the shallots and coat in all the juices. Add the ginger, spices and chilli and cook gently.

Stir in stock, coconut milk, sugar and lime. Add the garlic. Simmer gently for 20mins.

Cut the monkfish into meaty lumps, allowing approx. 3 chunks per bowl.

Gently lower into the soup with the mussels and cook for 5mins.

Slide the chorizo in just before serving to heat through.

Serve into deep bowl and sprinkle with chopped coriander or pineapple sage.

Serve with steaming couscous if you prefer to eat it as a hearty main course.

Vegetable soup with mixed beans and pistou

600g fresh haricot beans
500g french beans, chopped
    into 2cm lengths
600g broad beans
400g soya beans
4 carrots, peeled and diced
4 potatoes, peeled and diced
1 leek, peeled and diced
2 green celery sticks, diced
6 baby turnips, peeled and
    diced
2 courgettes, diced
3 large tomatoes, skinned,
    deseeded and diced
400g slice of pumpkin,
    peeled and chopped
1 large onion, peeled and
    studded with 5 cloves
400g vermicelli
3 bay leaves
5 sprigs of fresh thyme
5 sprigs of fresh rosemary
salt and pepper

pistou
6 cloves smoked garlic
1 large bunch of basil, stalks
    removed and washed if
    necessary
300g grated parmesan, 250g
    for the pistou, 50g to be
    kept to decorate the soup
olive oil

Put the onion and the shelled haricot beans in a pan with 4 times the quantity of water, bring to a boil, skim and simmer for 40mins.

Add all the other ingredients for the soup and cook for 30mins.

Take out the onion and the herbs.

Make a paste with the pistou ingredients, either in a blender or a pestle and mortar.

Put a spoon full of pistou into each bowl or in the base of a large soup terrine and pour over the soup.

Stir all the time and serve topped with remaining parmesan.

Wild rice and chicken gumbo

400g wild rice, washed and
drained at least twice. **Cooked
in 3 times its volume of salted
water - takes approx. 40mins**
4 free range chicken breasts,
   roasted in the oven with
   a little salt and pepper
   - chopped roughly
   once cooled
50g butter
25g flour
2 finely diced onions
3 sticks of green celery
   finely diced
3 finely diced carrots
1 finely diced leek
75g toasted almond slithers
1tsp salt
freshly ground black pepper
1ltr chicken stock
300ml cream
60ml dry sherry or white wine
chopped flat leaf parsley/
   coriander and or chives

Melt the butter and cook the onions, carrots, leeks, celery, until softened.

Add the flour, and stir in the chicken stock, add the sherry/ white wine, and stir until it starts to thicken.

Add the rice, cream and chicken and cook for a further 20mins.

Stir through the chopped herbs and serve.

TIP
This soup can be made chunkier, and be more of a main meal with hot crusty bread. If you are reheating this then it may need some more water as the rice continues to absorb the liquid. Delicious!

Simple vegetable stock

6 leeks, peeled and chopped
8 carrots, peeled and chopped
6 big sweet onions, peeled
   and chopped
3 fennel bulbs, trimmed and
   chopped
3 fresh bay leaves
2tsp caraway
8 cardamom, smashed to
   release the flavour
a small handful of lovage
the tops off of a celery
small stick of lemon grass
splash of olive oil
100ml white wine
4ltrs water

In a large stockpot, heat the oil and fry the vegetables until soft without colouring them. Add all the other ingredients and add the water. Simmer for 1hr.

Strain, taste and reduce further if necessary.

Chill and divide up into freezer boxes or bags, mark the quantity and freeze.

If you keep it in the fridge it will not keep more than 2 days.

Simple fish stock

2kg fish bits!
3 onions, peeled and
chopped
3 carrots, peeled and
chopped
a bunch of freshly ripped off
celery leaves or a handful
of lovage
2tsp pink peppercorns
1tsp black peppercorn
1tsp caraway seeds
8 cardamom pods smashed
to release the flavour
300ml Noilly Prat or dry
white wine
3ltrs water

Place all the ingredients in a large saucepan or stock pot with the water.

Bring slowly to a simmer and leave for 30mins, strain through muslin several times if necessary, taste, chill and freeze into several blocks ready for easy use.

If the flavour is too bland then return to the heat and reduce further.

TIP
freeze into 250ml bags and mark the quantity on them, it's the perfect way to take out the right amount, reducing waste.

Simple chicken stock

5kg chicken bones, skins
removed, organs and any
remaining flesh removed
a couple of chicken feet
Helpful if you're in
Barcelona as the have
chicken feet stalls in the
under cover market! How
handy is that? Not very
when you live in France!
5 carrots, peeled and
chopped
5 leeks, peeled and chopped
5 onions, peeled and
chopped
a small handful of lovage or
2 celery sticks, chopped
3 fresh bay leaves,
2 tsp black pepper
2 sprigs of sage
300ml dry white wine
lots of cold water
a bag of ice!

Again depending on how I feel or what the purpose is for the stock I either roast the bones with a splash of olive oil or I blanch the bones in a large pot of gently simmering water for 1hr. Add the ice and this way you will be able to remove the fat by skimming it off the top! It becomes cloudy and solid which is much easier to remove.

Add all the spices, herbs, wine and vegetables, simmer for 40mins, skimming occasionally. Turn off the heat and leave to rest for 20mins. This helps the impurities to sink to the bottom of the pan.

Ladle the stock through a muslin cloth over a strainer or use a Chinois.

Don't use the cloudy stock at the bottom or it will defeat the whole careful ladling process in order to get a clear stock.

Taste and reduce down further to intensify the flavour if you wish.

Chill and freeze as for the other stocks or keep for a couple of days in the fridge.

SHOP. COOK. EAT.

Simple shellfish stock

2 crayfish or lobster shells,
    heads, claws etc., no flesh
    or innards
3 onions peeled and chopped
3 carrots peeled and chopped
10 tomatoes, chopped
a glass of Cognac - for the pot!
good glug of Noilly Prat or
    white wine
2 fennel bulbs
2 sticks smashed lemon grass
3 sprigs of tarragon

In a large stockpot, heat the oil and fry the shellfish until they start to colour, add the vegetables (not the tomatoes) and continue to cook and sizzle. Add the Cognac and flambé - watch your fingers! Add the Noilly Prat or white wine or both. Add all the herbs, spices and tomatoes.

Pummel the stockpot contents with a heavy wooden spoon, or rolling pin to extract lots of lovely flavours. Cover the contents with water and bring to a simmer for 30mins. Strain through a muslin lined sieve or use a Chinois, return to the pan and reduce down for 30mins, taste, chill and freeze or store in the fridge until needed but not more than 2 days.

Simple veal stock

ask your butcher for a bag of
    veal bones or beef approx.
    5kg or more!
1 calves foot or 3 or 4 pieces
    of oxtail
10 carrots, peeled and
    chopped
6 onions, peeled and
    chopped
6 leeks, peeled and chopped
10 tomatoes, chopped
5 sticks of celery chopped
big handful of parsley
6 fresh bay leaves
20 sprig fresh thyme
3tsp smashed juniper berries
3 star anise
6 cloves garlic, smashed
2 bottles of red wine
lots of water

Depending on how I feel I either roast the bones with a glug of olive oil and the onions until the are caramelized - but not burnt!

or

I blanch the bones in a large pan of simmering water for 1.5hrs skimming the frothy grey skin that floats to the top of the pan, then drain and wash off the impurities leaving the bones smooth.

Either way, I start the stock with a large clean pan. Into that add the bones and then lots, at least 6ltrs of water and the wine. When that comes to a simmer add the rest of the spices and vegetables.

Let the stock simmer for a least 4 hours and skim off the impurities every so often.

Ladle the stock out of the pan through a muslin cloth into a large bowl. Cool quickly and divide into bags of 250ml, label and freeze or keep in a stock box in the fridge until needed.

The stock can be reduced to intensify the flavour whenever you need to.

Pâtés, parfaits, terrines and potted meats

"The aroma of an eye catching terrine will make your mouth water"

Michel Roux

Although I actually learnt all my potted meats, pâtés, parfaits and terrine skill in France, it has always reminded me of dishes that we used to have for afternoon tea as a child. Every country has its own traditions regarding utilizing the entire beast - waste not want not my Granny used to say. It's a shame that so many people are squeamish of using some of the most nutritious parts of an animal, have you ever wondered where they go? In the UK for example any part of a pig or chicken that the English wouldn't use is sent to France!

It's true that in our Supermarkets one rarely sees, oxtail, pig cheeks, brawn or junket. Specialist shops might now supply a real Cockerel if you're lucky!

The French markets are awash with body parts that the modern English person would run away from, hand over mouth. Totally uneducated! Ask anyone over a certain age and they will reply nostalgically referring to the black pudding they got for breakfast on Sundays, roast potatoes made with real dripping, a total no go now thanks to public health warnings regarding heart attacks and obesity. But, I totally disagree, so long as it is in moderation, that's the problem - one must display self-control.

I have to mention though that whilst in Barcelona, I was astonished to see the main market just off, Las Rambles, was heaving with market stalls piled high with skinned sheep heads, others with various animals stomachs, cockerels claws (seriously, what is there to eat on a cockerel's claw?). This is where even I just stood motionless, mouth open, when a 5ltr water bottles (in a past life), full of what I assume to be pigs blood, were wheeled on a trolley and deposited behind the counter of the butcher. Can't really see that happening at Borough Market in London!

I could never be a vegetarian, but I do have difficulties with animal welfare, so if I have bought my pig from my neighbour and its life has been extinguished to put food on my table, why would I waste the best bits?

I might not actually like them myself, but I know worthy souls who would love a freshly bbq'd tripe sausage or braun terrine with garden tomato salad.

I have looked for recipes that I would use and enjoy along with getting it past my kids. Pâtés, potted meats, parfaits and creamy fish terrines have been made for centuries, a farmhouse staple for a quick lunch, or a delicate dish at the most elegant restaurants and they are perfect for bringing out the intense flavour of the meat or fish used. With the parfaits I cook them on low heat in a bain marie for a relatively short time, they will be laced with a little alcohol and not too much else as the flavour is to be delicate, smooth and perfectly cooked. Farmhouse coarse pâtés cooked for much longer with stronger flavours, in them I would use the hearts, liver and kidneys as no one in my house would eat them on their own.

Mackerel in a creamy Dijon mustard sauce is my take on a relative cheap dish of cooked fish with a mustard sauce, but this recipe includes, lemon zest and dill resulting in a refreshing potted fish ideal for spooning over a salad or just to enjoy with crusty bread and some cherry tomatoes.

The most enlightening preserving of meats, however, was when I discovered 'rillettes' known to us as potted meat, simply a meat spread cooked for many hours in its own fat, drained and shredded with a fork, seasoned and potted in jars or terracotta pots with a light layer of melted fat poured on top to preserve it.

It really is one of the most delicious things I have ever eaten.

I tend to mix my pork rillettes with a couple of duck legs, as I find the pork a little too fatty, of course I had to tweak the recipe and add a few star anise, a crust of cassia bark and some lightly crushed juniper berries, just to give it a slightly more complex flavour.

For a delicate rillette I choose lightly home smoked salmon, combining 2 of my favourite methods. No cooking is necessary for the salmon once it has been smoked, shredded into large flakes, seasoned with some black pepper and a quick zap of lemon zest is all it needs. Served on soda bread with a crème fraîche (or sour cream) and horseradish dressing laced with capers is ideal for a light lunch, picnic or as a starter with a fresh leafed salad bouquet with viola flowers.

Poached foie gras 'au tourchon'

2 x 600g foie gras -
free range of course!

for the marinade
2½tsp salt
1tsp white pepper
1tsp sugar
1tbsp of each Cognac,
Madeira and Port
cheesecloth to wrap the foie
gras in approx. 1m long
and 50cm wide
pinch of ground mace

a large quantity of water or
chicken stock - enough to
poach the foie gras
it's best to have a fish kettle
ready to use as a poacher

Take the lobes and place on a clean tea towel. Separate the lobes, slice them into four lengthways to tease out the nerves and veins that run through them – it takes a little practise but it's easy enough to do.

Prepare a large bowl with iced water and soak the lobes with 4tbsp of salt to draw out the excess blood that might then stain the finished pâté. Soak for a few hours or over night.

Drain the lobes and pat dry with a clean tea towel. Sprinkle over the seasoning and drizzle over the alcohols, break up the foie gras to form a loaf shape and place them in the centre of a large piece of baking parchment roll up the parchment to make a cylinder approx. 40cm long and 10cm in diameter.

Unwrap the foie gras and lay it on the cheesecloth then wrap it tightly up twisting the ends to make sure the foie gras is wrapped securely. Tie with string and make a loop at one end so it is easy to hang up after poaching.

Knot the foie gras every 3cm all the way along.

In a large pan of simmering water or chicken stock, gently lower the foie gras in it and poach for 4mins, and then remove and plunge into iced water to stop the cooking process.

Place the foie gras onto a clean tea towel and wrap up securing at each ends as before. Hang the foie gras in the fridge overnight. The next day unwrap the foie gras and cut into discs.

Serve with a leafy salad bouquet and one of my delicious pickles or salsa's.

Smoked mackerel pâté with freshly grated horseradish

500g freshly smoked
  mackerel, kippers or any
  other smoked fish
5cm fresh horseradish root,
  it doesn't keep for too
  long, but it's definitely
  worth getting some for
  this recipe
65g soft unsalted butter
100g crème fraîche
juice and zest of 1 lemon
freshly ground black pepper
  and possibly a pinch
  of salt
small bunch of chopped
  fresh dill

In a large bowl, shred the mackerel, grate the horseradish, add the lemon zest - mash the contents with a fork.

Add the butter and the rest of the ingredients, mix again to form a rough paste, taste and adjust the seasoning.

Chill over night in the fridge.

Serve with olive oil biscuits, chilled papaya and mango salsa with an extra twist of lime juice and extra chilli!

Mackerel in Dijon mustard sauce

5 whole mackerel
1 lemon, juice and rind
1tbsp Dijon mustard
200g crème fraîche
freshly ground black pepper
pinch of flaky sea salt
good quality olive oil

Put the mackerel fillets in a sheet of foil on a baking tray. Spritz with olive oil, a small pinch of sea salt and freshly cracked pepper. Wrap tightly and bake in a hot oven for 10mins then take out and open parcel. Cool.

In a bowl add all the other ingredients and mix well, taste and adjust the seasoning. Carefully put the mackerel fillets in the sauce, stir gently, the fish will break up a little and then pot in your Kilner jars or any other serving dish and chill until very cold.

Serve with olive oil crackers, warm crunchy bread and salad.

Smoked salmon rillette

to smoke the salmon
100g sea salt flakes
6tbsp light brown sugar
**8 fresh responsibly sourced
    salmon fillets – skin on**

to marinade the salmon
300ml bourbon
300ml maple syrup
3tsp dijon mustard
4tbsp light brown sugar
**1tsp fresh ground black
    pepper**
or see p.48

to finish
zest of 1 lemon
freshly ground black pepper
30g horseradish
**a small bunch of freshly
    chopped dill**

Mix the salt and sugar together and rub generously over the salmon fillets. Cover tightly with cling film and chill for several hours.

Put all the marinade ingredients in a saucepan and heat until the sugar has dissolved. Cool.

Take out the salmon fillets and rinse off all the salt/sugar mix, pat dry. Cut several slices in the sides of the salmon, place in a dish and pour over ¾ of the marinade. Cover completely and chill again for several hours.

Prep the smoker according to manufacture's instructions. Smoke fillets for 15-25mins (depending on the thickness of the fillets) glazing several times with remaining marinade.

Turn off smoker after 25mins and leave to rest for 20mins. Take out of the smoker and gently shred with the prongs of a fork.

Stir through the remaining ingredients and taste. Adjust the seasoning, transfer to a pretty jar and chill until needed.

Serve with crunchy salad and a delicious cucumber and citrus salsa on olive oil crackers or crusty bread.

Country pâté

3.5kg coarsely minced belly
free range pork
700g liver, heart & kidneys,
coarsely chopped – from
the pig
1kg coarsely chopped free
range veal, or turkey
5 large onions, roughly
chopped
6 cloves garlic, chopped
300g roughly chopped flat
leaf parsley
4 free range eggs
50ml Cognac
50ml port
30ml madeira
4 whole cloves
10g juniper berries
10g red baie
15g thyme – dried or 30g
fresh (no stalks)
30g coarse sea salt
12 bay leaves
12 sage leaves
12 twigs fresh thyme
12 squares pig skin or
6 rashers of bacon cut
in half
3tsp mixed spice

Pre-heat oven to 180°C, 350°F. You will need 2 terrine dishes
with lids or a selection of preserving jars with rubber seals.

Using a blender on pulse, roughly chop the onions and
garlic, holding 2 onions back. Pulse quickly the remaining 2
onions with the parsley but do not blend for long or the
parsley will become a purée.

In a pestle and mortar crush the cloves, juniper berries and
the red baies until moist. In a very large mixing bowl or clean
washing up bowl mix all the ingredients together with your
hands until the herbs and spices are evenly mixed through
the meats.

Divide the mixture between your Terrine dishes or your
preserving jars. Top with a leaf of sage, bay, thyme and a
square of pig fat or bacon.

Place the terrines with their lids on a deep roasting pan and
fill ¾ of the way up with hot water. Cook slowly for at last
2.5-3hrs. Remove and cool before chilling in the fridge.

Serve with home pickled gherkins and crunchy farmhouse bread.

TIPS
*Oven baked pâté will have a more caramelized flavour than
the Kilner jars. Both are delicious, but really do have a totally
different flavour.*

*The Kilnar jars are brilliant for an impromptu supper or
summer lunch, so if you do decide to use them, pack the raw
ready mixed up pâté into the jars, place a piece of bacon/ pig
skin on top with a few herbs, Put the rubber seal on the lid,
shut and follow manufacturers instructions. This recipe should
make enough for 12.*

*They will need to be cooked for 2.5hrs. Take out of water when
cold, test to see the seal is tightly shut and store until needed for
up to 2 years.*

Chicken liver pâté with baby vegetables pickled in honey and fig vinegar

for the baby veg
½ cucumber
16 small white onions
    peeled
16 cauliflower florets washed
2 carrots peeled

for the marinade
4tbsp any local honey
5tbsp honey and fig vinegar
1tbsp salt
10g white mustard seeds
2 flowering fennel heads
    or 1tsp fennel seeds

for the pâté
900g chicken livers, free
    range, and cleaned
10 shallots, chopped finely
small knob of butter for
    cooking shallots
3 cloves garlic, peeled and
    smashed to a pulp
1tsp lemon thyme leaves
100ml Cognac
200ml madeira
200ml port
850g unsalted butter,
    melted, impurities
    spooned off the top
10 free range eggs
3tsp salt and 1tsp ground
    white pepper

Peel the cucumber and make ribbons using a vegetable peeler. When you arrive at the seeds stop! Repeat for the carrots.

In a saucepan boil 1¾ltrs of water with 1tbsp salt. Blanch onions for 5mins. After 3mins add the cauliflower and carrots. Drain and pat dry. Mix marinade ingredients together except for the honey and mix in veg. Leave to pickle for 2 days then drain and mix with the honey. It will keep well for a week, but will then start to loose it's colour.

Preheat oven to 150°C, 300°F. In a saucepan sweat shallots and garlic in 1tsp butter. Add the Cognac, madeira and port. Bring to the boil, reduce down to approx. 150ml. Chill.

Make sure all the liver is trimmed free of gall and puree the lot for 1min in a food processor. Add the shallot and madeira mixture to the puréed liver. Blend for a few seconds. Add eggs and salt, Blend again. Pass through a sieve using the back of a ladle to force it through. This removes any strands of gall that might be left. Place the mixture in terrine dish or individual serving jars/ramekins and cover with buttered paper, then foil.

Cook in a roasting pan lined with foil for 1hr 20mins for the large ones and 35mins for the small ones. Pouring enough hot water into the roasting pan to come ¾ up the sides of the dishes.

Once cooked leave to cool and cover with a little melted fat to avoid discolouration. Keep in fridge one day before serving to let the flavours develop. Turn out and slice or serve with pickled veg.

The pâté can be enriched by replacing ¼ livers for foie gras.

Smoked salmon mousse with oyster juice and coriander infused jelly

8 inox rings
enough smoked salmon to
   get 24 discs as large as the
   inox rings
500g smoked salmon
   trimmings (use trimmings
   from the disc)
½tsp cayenne pepper
1 lemon
500ml whipping cream
sea salt and white pepper
250ml fish stock
50ml salt water taken from
   the juice of opened oysters
1 small bunch of fresh
coriander – leaves only
3 leaves of gelatine soaked
   in cold water for 5mins
   – drain well
4 slices of brioche

Using the 500g smoked salmon blend until smooth in a food processor with the juice of the lemon, cayenne pepper, salt and pepper. When smooth, very slowly pour in ½ of the whipping cream. Pass the mixture through a sieve to remove any sinew and chill for 5mins. Whip the remaining cream to form soft peaks and fold gently into the mousse.

In a small saucepan bring the fish stock and oyster water to the boil. Take off the heat and stir in the gelatine leaves – leave to cool until nearly set.

Line the inox rings with greaseproof paper and place a salmon disc in the base of each ring. Pipe the salmon mousse evenly around the base and place a second disc on top.

Pipe another layer of mousse on top of that and top with a third disc. Spoon a small amount of the chilled nearly set sea water over the top of each mousse and chill.

Press 3 coriander leaves in a circle over each mousse and spoon the remaining sea water over the top to seal the leaves in – chill for several hours.

Serve on a small plate with thinly toasted strips of brioche.

Alternatively you can mix your own home smoked fresh salmon for the mousse with the discs being shop bought smoked salmon.

Canapés

"I am not a glutton –
I am an explorer
of food"

Erma Bombeck

How else can you describe a sea of canapés that spread out before you as far as the eye can see?

Other then a taste of loveliness tempting us on to the next delightful mouthful of exploding flavours. If you want to impress then canapés are a jolly good way to start.

Deciding what canapés to make is the hardest thing. With access to a world of different flavours and styles, I do have to stop myself getting carried away and end up making vast amount of endless different types. I can't resist them.

I always find creating a selection of really beautiful, amazingly presented ones is essential. You'll be guaranteed a wow from all the guests, but it's also a very good idea to have some simpler more boot filling varieties too.

Giving yourself time to prepare is my mantra. I know it's a bore, but a relaxed hostess means the party will be so much more fun!

Music on, roll up your sleeves and enjoy the creative moment. Stick to the order of work and try not to get distracted.

Making the bases for the canapés can always be done way ahead of tie and frozen. Gougeres, warm cheesy puffs of air can be made ahead and frozen uncooked. Popped in the oven 20min before needed and they are perfect, piled generously high on wooden platters.

Giant twisted caraway and cheddar straws are perfect for freezing. Cooked from frozen they ease the pressure that inevitable hosts and hostesses feel as guests are due to arrive. Blinis can be frozen or popped in the fridge, warmed in the oven before piling high with crayfish and mango cocktail decorated with dill fronds.

Picking out some jars of pesto from the larder, cracking open preserved duck rillettes or tasting the first pear and tomato salsa from your latest batch will all add to the ease of achieving sublime perfectly proportioned loveliness. Mission accomplished and definitely time for a well deserved cocktail.

Citrus crayfish and avocado cocktail

**400g fresh crayfish tails,
  cook and chopped. Shrimp/
  prawns can be used also**
**small quantity of lemon
  mayonnaise recipe *but*
  made with lime juice**
1tsp lemon grass pulp
**3 ripe avocados, peeled
  and diced**
zest of 2 limes
juice of 1 lemon
pinch of paprika
small bunch of fresh dill
**1 ripe mango, peeled and
  finely diced**
**1 pink grapefruit, cut into
  segments then finely diced**
black pepper and salt
**a mixture of fresh variegated
  salad leaves shredded
  finely**
**1 fresh red chilli, deseeded
  and finely chopped**

In a bowl, mix the chopped crayfish tails with enough lime mayonnaise to make a thick mixture, stir in the lime zest, some chopped dill and lemon grass pulp. Season with salt and pepper, taste.

In a separate bowl, mix the finely diced avocados with a pinch of paprika, lemon juice, garlic, salt and pepper.

To complete the cocktail
In a small canapés dish place a small quantity of shredded salad leaves followed by a spoon of avocado, topped with the lime crayfish cocktail, decorate with a few mango and pink grapefruit dices, a frond of dill and a couple of diced red chillis.

This dish can be made bigger and served as a starter.

Coriander, mint and cucumber raita

**2 fresh chillis, red or green,
  seeds out or in!**
**2 large handfuls of
  coriander and 2 of mint,
  roughly chopped**
1 onion, chopped
**1tbsp freshly squeezed
  lemon juice**
1tsp salt
**1 cucumber peeled and
  coarsely grated**
500ml natural yoghurt
**a large pinch of ground
  cumin**
**a pinch of freshly ground
  black pepper**
a pinch of chilli powder

Blend (excluding the cucumber) until a thick paste is formed.

Put the cucumber in a sieve and sprinkle with salt. Leave for 30mins to draw out the water.

Rinse off the salt from the cucumber and squeeze out and pat dry. Stir through the paste.

Store in a jar and chill in the fridge for a max. of 3 days.

Perfect with popadoms, warm pitta bread or raw vegetables.

SHOP. COOK. EAT.

Hummus with roasted chick peas and pine nuts

**500g dried chick peas,
   soaked over night in a
   twice their volume of cold
   water with 80g
   bicarbonate of soda
   (bicarb is optional, it just
   makes them softer) for at
   least 12 hours**
5 cloves garlic
2tsp salt
3tsp ground cumin
juice of 4 lemons
**100ml olive oil (you might
   need some more)**
**100ml tahini (optional with
   this recipe)**

60ml olive oil
3 smashed cloves garlic
80g whole chick peas
50g pine nuts
**juice of 1 lemon maybe
   more**
**sea salt and freshly ground
   pepper**
1tsp cumin seeds

Cook the chick peas in salted water for 2hrs until tender
at a low temperature. They don't want to be mush, but soft
when you press them.

When cool enough to handle pick out the husky skins that
you will see floating on the top of the water, then drain and
set 80g of whole chic peas to one side.

In a food processor add all the other ingredients and razz to
a paste, add a little water if it's too think or more lemon
juice, but taste before hand.

Taste and add more garlic, salt, lemon or pepper if you think
it needs it. I think it's more about taste and texture than
following the recipe to the letter!

For the garnish
Heat up a the remaining olive oil in frying pan and and add
the reserved chic peas, pine nuts, garlic and cumin seeds, fry
until coloured but not so that the garlic is bitter.

Squeeze in the lemon juice and pour over the hummus.

Taramasalata

**5 slices white bread,
   no crusts**
⅓ cup milk
100g smoked cod's roe
1 egg yolk
½ grated onion
1 clove garlic, crushed
2tbsp lemon juice
⅓ cup olive oil
white pepper

Blend everything together. Chill.

*Try and source smoked cod's roe, it's definitely worth it.
Nothing else will do!*

Olive oil biscuits

300g plain flour
1tsp baking powder
120ml water
30ml olive oil
pinch of sea salt
1tsp aromatic salt or some
  green masala paste
pinch of cracked black
  pepper
flaky sea salt for serving

In a mixing bowl or electric mixer, blend all the ingredients together (not the flaky sea salt) to form a soft dough. When the dough is smooth wrap in cling film and chill for 2hrs.

Take out of fridge and pinch out 2cm pieces and roll into balls. Using a floured rolling in roll each ball out as thinly as possible and place on a baking tray lined with non stick baking parchment. Chill again.

Brush with olive oil and sprinkle over the flaky sea salt. Bake at 200°C, 400°F until golden, approx. 5mins.

Rosemary and parmesan biscuits

120g butter
100g grated parmesan
1tbsp chopped rosemary
150g plain flour
pinch of aromatic spice
  or salt

Blend all the ingredients together, in a food processor.

Wrap in clingfilm and chill for 1hr.

Cut the dough in half and roll it out between 2 sheets of clingfilm. Cut out biscuit shapes.

Preheat the oven to 180°C, 350°F.

Place the biscuits on a baking tray lined with non stick baking parchment cook 15mins.

Kim's blue cheese biscuits

120g blue cheese or a
  mixture of blue cheese
  and parmesan
120g flour (use rice flour to
  make them gluten free)
pinch cayenne
120g butter - grated
1 egg yolk

Crumble cheese. Sift in flour and cayenne. Add yolk and work into a dough.

Refrigerate for a few hours. Roll into small balls, flatten a bit with a fork and put a piece of walnut on top.

Bake at 180°C, 350°F for about 12mins.

Giant cheese straws and fresh white anchovy straws

1.5kg puff pastry, rolled out into 60x40cm or as big as your oven will allow to cook comfortably
20g Dijon mustard
50ml milk
6 egg yolks
25g aromatic salt mix
20g caraway seeds, maybe a little more
500g grated cheese, mature and tangy

Oven 180°C, 350°F Roll out all the pastry into sheets and stack up on a baking tray, chill for 1hr in fridge.

In a bowl mix the egg yolks, milk, aromatic salt and Dijon mustard. Brush with the egg wash and sprinkle the cheese over, pat down with your hands to make it stick. Flip over and repeat. Return to the fridge for another ½hr.

Take out and cut the pastry into lengths. Pick the straw up with both hands twist into a spiral. Place on a lined baking sheets and bake in the oven for 25mins or until golden brown.

If they come out of the oven looking slightly crunchy at the ends take a sharp knife and cut through the ends quickly without dragging the knife through them and it will leave a clean crisp edge!

for anchovy straws

300g tub fresh white anchovy's soaked in oil and garlic
5 egg yolks
2tsp Dijon mustard
a splash of milk for the egg wash

Roll out the pastry as before – place the sheet long ways across. Mix egg yolks, mustard and milk. Brush with the egg wash. Line the pastry with anchovies approx., starting 2cm from the left hand side and running down, and then do 2cm from the right hand side running down.

Start in the middle, running down and then approx. twice more to the left and then the right creating even lines from top to bottom at equal lengths apart without over-crowding.

Cover the first sheet of anchovy puff pastry with a second sheet. Press gently down between the lines of anchovies and chill for ½hr in the fridge. Take out and cut straws from side to side. The straws should be dotted with small pieces of anchovies. Cook until golden brown and risen approx. 25mins.

Blini's

See p.68

Goats cheese mousse with garlic tuiles

600g fresh goats cheese,
    preferably St Maure
300g double cream
pinch of white pepper
pinch of ground cumin
1tbsp finely chopped flat leaf
parsley, chives or chervil
    or a mixture of all 3

tuiles
50g plain flour
50g sugar
50g grated parmesan
1tsp salt
100g butter whisked until in
    looks like mayonnaise
1 egg white
2tsp garlic, crushed
1tsp finely chopped
    rosemary

Put all the ingredients into a blender, except for the herbs and blend until smooth. Transfer to a bowl, stir through the finely chopped herbs and chill until needed. Keep some chervil fronds for decorating.

Garlic tuiles
In a bowl mix the egg white into the flour, salt and sugar. Slowly whisk in the butter, then and the cheese and garlic. The batter should be smooth.

On a large baking sheet covered in non stick baking parchment, spoon a small blob of the mixer into the top corner and using the back of the spoon spread to form a small disc. Repeat over the baking tray, but allow space for the discs to spread.

Preheat oven to 180°C, 350°F. Bake until golden, carefully remove from the tray and place on a wire rack, place over a rolling pin to make curves or carefully but quickly wrap over an upside down muffin or dariole mould to form a cup.

Pipe the goats cheese mousse onto or into the garlic tuiles and decorate with some extra sprigs of chervil.

Fried ricotta cakes

500g ricotta
50g grated parmesan plus
    a little extra for serving
2tbsp plain flour
salt and pepper
1 large free range egg +
    1 extra yolk
splash of olive oil and knob
    of butter for frying
1tbsp freshly chopped herbs
1 finely chopped red chilli
    (if you like it hot) *or*
    1 finely chopped
    green chilli

Mix the ricotta, egg and extra yolk, parmesan, salt and pepper and the flour. Chill for 30mins.

In a large sauté pan heat up a splash of olive oil and butter and drop small spoonfuls of the mixture into the hot pan.

Fry until golden brown then flip over and do the same.

Serve immediately with a drizzle of olive oil or mandarin scented olive oil, sprinkling of sea salt and a little more parmesan or some tangy tomato and pear salsa - Super delicious!

Canapé gougères

125ml water
125ml milk
100g butter, diced
pinch of salt
1tsp sugar
150g plain flour, sifted twice
onto greaseproof paper
4 medium free range eggs,
brake into a bowl &
whisk with a fork to get
gloopy bubbles
40g gruyere cheese, grated
or you can use a stronger
cheese like cheddar
1tsp Dijon mustard

Preheat oven to 220°C, 425°F. Melt the butter in a saucepan with the milk, water, salt and sugar.

Bring to a frothy simmer, (no need to keep stirring it), for just a minute then take off the heat and tip in the flour which has been sifted onto the greaseproof paper.

Mix slowly together with a wooden spoon, at this stage it will look gloopy and a bit like wallpaper paste, don't panic.

Return to the hob over a low heat to dry out the mixture, stir firmly. It should be smooth and just pull away from the sides when dry enough, less than a 1min.

Turn the pastry into a large mixing bowl. Steady the bowl on a tea towel and start adding the eggs approx. 1 at a time and beat really well in between times. You are trying to incorporate as much air into them as possible – it is a dig and lift action, rather than a round and round action, best achieved by holding the bowl under the crook of one's arm! Beat until shiny and smooth.

Fold in the cheese and mustard - Do not beat any more or you will knock the air out.

Spoon or pipe into small blobs on greaseproof paper on a baking tray.

Glaze with egg glaze and bake in the oven until well risen, approx. 20mins then reduce the temperature right down for another 5mins to dry out the pastry.

Serve warm with drinks or stuff with delicious fillings

Truffle custard with lemon and chive tuiles

If you are using real egg shells you will need one shell for each guest or you can use another vessel or fake egg shells like me!
4 eggs
300ml milk
450ml double cream
Salt and white pepper
1tsp truffle oil or lemon oil if you find the truffle oil too strong in flavour

Warm the cream and milk together then blend everything in a food processor until smooth.

Divide between the egg shells or other serving vessel and cook in a bain marie in the oven at 150°C, 300°F for 45mins or until set.

Keep warm and serve with a lemon and chive tuile.

Lemon and chive tuiles

2 large potatoes peeled and chopped into a rectangle
5cm lengths of chive
grated zest of 1 lemon, dried to a fine powder and mixed with a tsp of flaked salt
large baking sheet
3tsp melted butter

Slice the potatoes as finely as possible using a mandolin.

Brush the baking sheet with butter and cover with potato slices place a length of chive in the middle of each slice and top with another slice of potato, press down firmly with finger to make sure it sticks, sprinkle with lemon salt.

Brush a 2nd piece of greaseproof paper with butter and place this butter side down on the potato tuiles.

Weigh the potatoes down with a 2nd baking tray with weights on and bake for 15-20mins turning the baking tray over halfway through cooking to keep the colour even.

This will take some practice, but it's worth it.

Black pudding with buttered Cognac apples

500g freshly made black
   pudding with the skin on
5 cooking apples if possible,
   or any other sharp apple
   that goes soft when it is
   cooked, peeled cored
   and diced
a large glug of Cognac
60g butter
1 soup spoon of brown
   sugar
1 sprig of lemon thyme,
   normal will do if not
small quantity of smooth
   Dijon mustard
approx. 20cm pastry discs,
   toasted bread circles or
   filo pastry baskets

Preheat the oven to 180°C, 350°F.

Fry the apples in hot butter with a spoon of sugar and the sprig of thyme until starting to caramelise, pour in the Cognac and flambé.

The apples are ready when they start to break up - add a little water if necessary.

Cut the cold black pudding into 1cm pieces and place each one on a small pastry disc or any of the other choices of bases.

Warm in the oven for 10mins, remove and decorate with a spoon of apples and a dot of Dijon mustard.

Little pots of foie gras brulée

385ml double cream or
   crème fraîche
300g foie gras pâté
6 egg yolks
2tsp port
2tsp madère
pinch of salt and white
   pepper

Preheat oven to 120°C, 250°F. Mix all the ingredients together in a food processor, sieve and divide between small ramekin dishes.

Bake in a 'bain-marie' on a low setting for 20mins, cool.

Sprinkle with a little soft brown sugar and burn to a crackle with a blow torch.

Serve with a small olive oil biscuit.

Spiced honey bread with onion confit and warm foie gras

1 loaf of spiced honey bread
200g foie gras pâté
1 quantity of onion confit
   (see p.131)
flakes of sea salt

Cut the spiced honey bread into slim rectangles - try and get 2 out of each slice. Don't waste the trimmings, turn into crumbs and freeze – they can be used in a crumble topping.

Place the spiced bread on a baking tray and place a spoonful of the onion confit on top.

Cut a small slice of pâte – the same size as the spiced bread and put on top of the onion.

Place in the oven for 5-10mins until the pâte starts to shine – don't let in melt.

Sprinkle with some flaked sea salt and serve warm.

Starters

> *To eat is a
> necessity, but to eat
> intelligently is an art.*
> *La Rochefoucauld*

Traditionally the French hors d'oeuvres were probably main courses, but became more of something to wet ones appetite for the courses to come. I like to think of this as a truism. But, having tasted so many succulent and perfectly balanced flavours in a starter, I sometimes wish it were promoted back to the main course. Or at least a main course for a light and sociable lunch what we now fashionably call 'al fresco'!

I actually think that starters are a chance to shine, and I love preparing them simply because I really feel the pressure as the main course looms. People look towards the so called "star of the show - the main event" leaving the starter somewhat in the shadow as the warm up act but I truly believe it creates a marvellous opportunity to really go to town resulting in a delightful gem with guests wanting more!

When I was invited to spend time in 3* Michelin L'Esperance Chez Marc Meaneau, I was allowed to wander freely, to choose any work station I was interested in. Only being there for a short time, I didn't feel it appropriate to elbow in on a teams tightly run system, but I chose to observe how each section functioned. The cold starters was one of my favourite places to watch as they methodically prepared the freshly delivered ingredients. It was clearly apparent as the service started that the pressure was not the same as for mains or hot starters.

The preparation was just as intricate but the delivery was planned ahead and tweaked just before serving. Which led me to suggest to my own students and in general conversation when quizzed about the pressure of serving that pressure is avoidable with forethought and a well planned menu!

In my humble opinion I do not believe that a Chef can excel in every aspect of a meal, we all have our weak points or perhaps are slightly less passionate about certain ingredients than others. I for one am the first to admit that I put myself under pressure when preparing to serve 200 hot medium rare duck breasts in cherry sauce for example. I can do it, I know I can do it, but the pressure is there all the same; once it is all served on hot plates looking fabulous it's a huge relief and I am left wondering what all the worry was about, but with a starter it is a perfect way to master new ideas, to spend time

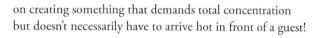

on creating something that demands total concentration but doesn't necessarily have to arrive hot in front of a guest!

It can also just be something simple, totally delicious, beautifully presented, just honest 'crudites' style a light pre cursor to something even more sublime. Simple and discreet or a big wham of flavour, the choice is yours, so when planning the menu if the starter is big the main should be a calmer simpler affair. If your pressure point is hot mains, as mine is or hot starters or desserts, go for starters that are chilled and can be prepared in advance.

A delicate subtle starter full of fresh ingredients lends itself better appreciated before a stronger more complicated main course so just keep it simple!

Tomato tartare with freshly smoked mackerel and wild rocket

3 tomatoes, peeled, deseeded
   and finely chopped. You
   can also use confit
   tomatoes
flaked sea salt
1tsp olive oil
1tsp minced shallots
½tsp tomato vinegar
1tsp minced chives

500g freshly smoked
   mackerel, shredded
   into flakes
1 egg
2tbsp finely chopped
   fresh dill
500g fluffy warm mashed
   potatoes, mashed with no
   milk, just a knob of butter
freshly ground black pepper
90ml fresh cream
3 small shallot, finely diced
1tsp butter
grated zest of 1 lemon

for the crust
400g finely ground
   breadcrumbs
3 eggs, whisked with a fork
   in a shallow dish
60g flour
salt and pepper
rocket oil (see oils recipe)
   leek shoots, cress shoots
   or other similar fine
   frizzy leaf

For the tartare
Sprinkle the salt over the tomatoes and strain for 1hr to remove excess liquid. Dice finely - omit the salt part if using confit of tomatoes. Combine with all the ingredients and chill until needed.

For the smoked mackerel croquet
In a bowl, mix all the ingredients together apart from the crust ones. Create a firm ball with your hand. Divide up the mixture into balls approx. the size of a golf ball, set aside. Dust each ball in flour, shaking off the excess.

Dip each ball in egg, shaking of the excess then roll each one in breadcrumbs. Repeat the process of egg and breadcrumbs, pat into perfect balls and chill.

Heat up enough oil to immerse the balls and fry gently until golden, approx. 4mins. Repeat until all the fish is cooked, drain onto kitchen paper to remove the excess oil.

Take a large pastry cutter and place it in the middle of the plate spread a spoon of the tartare mixture around the ring, remove place one croquet in the centre and then decorate with a bunch of fine shoots.

Swirl round a ring of rocket oil and serve.

TIP
You could change the oil and use beetroot coulis or add a poached egg to the top of some delicious crunchy blanched green beans or switch the smoked mackerel croquet with a goats cheese croquet.

Winter beet confit with fresh goats cheese

2 yellow beets
2 purple beets
2 pink beets
500g fresh firm goats
cheese, drained if
necessary
pinch of salt and freshly
ground black pepper
1 tbsp finely chopped chives
mandarin oil
rocket (arugula) oil
olive oil
beetroot coulis (you will
need 2 purple beets
for this)
white balsamic vinegar
syrup or black balsamic
syrup if you cannot find
the white
fresh rocket to decorate

You will need a 3-4cm pastry cutter depending on the size of your beets.

For the beet coulis
Wrap the beets in foil and cook in the oven until soft. Skin them and puree with 1 tbsp of vinegar, taste and add more vinegar if necessary. Sieve the mixture into a clean jug. If the coulis is slightly too thick add a small spoon of water and mix.

Pour into a small plastic squeezy bottle to be used later – chill.

For the rocket (arugula) oil
In a small blender add ¾ cup of olive oil and a generous handful of clean arugula. Blend until smooth and bright green.

Pour into a small plastic squeezy bottle to be used later – chill.

For the beet confit
Wrap the beets individually in foil and roast for at least an hour in a medium oven or until a knife goes smoothly into the beets with no resistance. Take them out, cool, peel and slice into approx. 3mm slithers.

Keep all 3 colours separate to avoid running colours - chill.

For the goats cheese
In a bowl mush up the goats cheese with your fingers and add a pinch of salt, black pepper and the chopped chives.

With damp hands roll out small balls of goats cheese and place them on a tray lined with non stick paper or seram wrap – you need 3 per person. Chill in the fridge for 1hr.

To assemble
Prepare 8 medium sized plates.

Before placing 3 balls of goats cheese on your plate think about the design of your presentation. For square or rectangular try arranging them in a straight line. For a round try thinking about the beets in the middle and the goats cheese around the outside.

P.T.O.

Then using the rocket (arugula) oil make a small dot that will then spread slightly when you place your goats cheese on, repeat another 2 times. Think about the spacing and presentation.

Using alternate beets make up a small tower of approx. 6 discs high. Using the beetroot purée place a dot on top of the beets and decorate with a leaf of chervil. Dot the beetroot purée on the plate parallel to the goats cheese.

TIPS
You need to remember your portion control, so divide the weight of your goats cheese into 8 (that's how many you are making for) and then by 3 (for the 3 goats cheese ball per portion).

To achieve the professional look take the pastry cutter and cut out the perfect circle! How easy is that?!

Think about how restaurants often use much larger plates than necessary for the entrée – purely for presentation!

It makes a big difference than a crowded entrée plate.

Poached oysters in champagne

10 fresh No.3 oysters *or* 5pp, served on a bed of coarse sea salt to steady the shells
250ml of champagne, leaving enough for a couple of glasses in the bottle
4 egg yolks
250ml cream
2 shallots very finely chopped
white pepper
8 tarragon leaves
½ lemon

Chuck the oysters, over a bowl and a strainer, strain the oysters and pick out any shell – reserve the juice. Scrub the deepest half of the oyster shells and set 5 on each plate in the sea salt.

In a large shallow pan pour in the champagne, oyster juice and then the oysters. Gently warm the oysters through, do not let the liquid boil or even, come to a simmer – you should be able to pick then up with your fingers.

In a separate pan heat the cream, egg yolks tarragon and shallots. Season with white pepper and a squeeze of lemon.

Warm through, constantly turning until the sauce starts to thicken – immediately take of the heat. Spoon the oysters back into their shell and spoon the sauce over and serve.

Fresh halloumi with wild mushroom cream and fresh caraway brioche

3 x 50g halloumi or similar fresh cheese
1 loaf of freshly made or bought brioche
500g girolles mushrooms, fresh, dried or frozen
1 large glass chablis or alligote
3tbsp white wine or tarragon vinegar
500ml double cream
30g butter splash olive oil
3tsp caraway seeds
fresh chervil or flat leaf parsley
3 shallots finely chopped
3tsp red pepper corns
2 smashed smoked garlic cloves
salt and ground black pepper

Cut the brioche into squares, circles or rectangles and put on a baking tray.

Using your hands break up the halloumi and place chunks on each piece of brioche. Drizzle with olive oil, crush between your hands the red peppercorns whilst moving over the halloumi to scatter them over the top, sprinkle over the caraway seeds, salt and pepper – set aside until needed.

Preheat your oven to 180°C, 350°F. Meanwhile in a large frying pan melt the butter and a splash of olive oil. Add the shallots and soften, then add the mushrooms – remember if you are using dried mushrooms you have to soak them in warm water first for 30mins then drain and squeeze out the excess juice, keep the juice for soups it has a lovely wild flavour! Let the mushroom absorb all the liquid in the pan and then turn up the heat and add the vinegar.

Let all the liquid disappear and add the wine, reduce by half before adding the cream. Whilst this is reducing add your brioche and halloumi to the oven for 10mins. Season and taste the mushrooms. When the cream starts to thicken turn off the heat and stir through the herbs.

Take the brioche out of the oven and place on a serving platter or plate up as if to serve to your guests. Spoon over the mushroom cream and serve.

For an extra treat a small slice of foie gras on the halloumi just before spooning over the mushrooms is divine!

Scallops on a bed of tender green asparagus

**24 fresh scallops, coral
    removed and trimmed
1 lemon and 1 lime
50ml cream
50ml vegetable stock
36 young green asparagus,
    trimmed and delicately
    peeled, reserve 12 for
    decoration
300g fresh garden peas
a small bunch of fresh dill,
    stalks removed
1tsp grated ginger
1 shallot finely sliced
salt and freshly ground
white pepper
1tsp lemon salt
30g butter**

In a saucepan of salted boiling water cook the peas for 5mins
until tender, drain and refresh in iced water to seal their
colour.

In a small pan melt 1tsp butter and sweat the shallots until
they are soft but not coloured.

In a food processor add the peas, shallots, ginger, cream and
vegetable stock salt and pepper. Blend until smooth and
strain to remove any bits.

Blanch 24 of the asparagus in boiling salt water for 2mins,
drain and refresh in iced water.

Using a mandolin thinly slice lengthways the raw asparagus
and set aside.

Just before serving, warm through the petit pois coulis
whisking to a froth.

Pan fry the blanched asparagus in a little butter. Pan fry the
scallops for 1min each side.

To serve
On a plate place the asparagus, tips facing the same way, top
with 2 scallops and decorate with a pinch of lemon salt and
a twist of the raw asparagus. Swirl with a spoon or using
a plastic bottle the coulis of petit pois.

SHOP. COOK. EAT.

Poached eggs from Burgundy

1 egg per person for a
starter, 2 eggs for main
with salad
1 slice of french bread, cut
on the diagonal or slices
of fresh brioche or spiced
bread, 2 slices if you are
using 2 eggs
½tbsp olive oil, seasoned
with salt and pepper

sauce
1 bottle of red wine,
pinot noir
50ml deep beef stock
35g flour
35g butter + extra knob of
butter to whisk in at the end
1tbsp chopped onion
½ jar redcurrant jelly
2 fresh bay leaves
8 thyme branches or
2tsp dried
5 juniper berries, roughly
crushed
10 black pepper corns
roughly crushed

onion confit
2 large red onions, white is
fine if you don't have red,
finely sliced
extra juniper berries, bay
leaf, cinnamon stick and 3
star anise to be added to
the onion jam
splash of tarragon or white
wine vinegar and a glass
of white wine
olive oil and a knob of
butter for the onion jam
1heaped tbsp sugar

In a large saucepan half filled with water bring to a simmer and swirl with a spoon, gently crack in the eggs one at a time and poach for approx. 2mins, then lift gently out with a slotted spoon and transfer straight into a bowl of iced water leave for a moment then again, gently lift out and drain on kitchen paper. Set aside until needed. In a saucepan melt the butter, soften the tablespoon of onion and add the flour, cook for a few minutes.

Turn down the heat and slowly add the red wine and beef stock, whisking all the time, this will thicken the sauce to a pouring consistency, whisk in the redcurrant jelly.

Add the peppercorns, juniper berries, thyme and bay leaves simmer for 5mins.

Sieve the sauce and taste, adjust the seasoning and whisk in a small knob of butter.

In a frying pan cook the onions in the oil and butter until just starting to caramelise, sprinkle over the sugar and season with salt and pepper.

Add the rest of the spices and deglaze with the tarragon vinegar then the white wine. Cook until it starts to caramelise and resemble jam.

Drizzle the bread with the seasoned olive oil and toast in the oven on both sides until golden brown.

Pan fry the lardons until they start to turn crispy, drain and set aside. Alternatively use pancetta and crisp up in the oven in whole strips *or* use fresh chorizo saucisson.

To serve, spoon the onions on the croutons, place an egg on the onions and warm in the oven for 1min.

Reheat the lardons in the oven for 1min. warm the sauce through and pour over the top of the egg until it is well covered and is spilling over the sides.

Sprinkle the parsley over the eggs, dot the reheated lardons around the plate and serve immediately.

PTO

finishing off
300g smoked lardons,
**   cooked until caramelized**
3tbsp fresh flat leaf parsley
**   or chervil, chopped**
sea salt and freshly ground
**   pepper**

Here's a twist!

White wine version
Make up as the red wine sauce, see how it totally changes the dish!

1 bottle of burgundian
**   white wine or any other**
**   chardonnay ¾ for the pot**
**   one for the chef!**
50ml vegetable/chicken
**   stock**
35g flour
35g butter + extra knob of
**   butter to whisk in at the**
**   end handful of fresh**
**   marjorie, stalks removed**
3 fresh bay leaves
freshly ground white pepper
1 soup spoon of white
**   balsamic syrup or maple**
**   syrup or honey**
5 crushed juniper berries
splash of cream

Tartare of wild salmon with miso dressing

1kg wild salmon fillet, skin
   and bones removed
1tsp dijon mustard
4tsp créme fraiche
zest and juice of 1 lemon
salt and white pepper
½tbsp chopped fresh dill

marinade
2tbsp fresh chopped dill or
   dried if fresh is
   unavailable
zest of 1 lemon
2tbsp salt and 2 of sugar

salad
1 cucumber peeled and
   finely sliced into rounds
1 quantity miso dressing
(see p.51)

garnish
200g créme fraiche
fresh dill
black lumpfish roe, caviar or
   slithers of lemon flesh and
   red peppercorns

Ask your fishmonger to skin, fillet and bone the wild fresh salmon.

In a bowl, mix up the marinade ingredients and rub them all over the salmon both sides. Wrap tightly in cling wrap and place in a shallow dish, refridgerate for 12hrs.

Unwrap and wash off marinade then pat dry with kitchen paper or a clean tea towel. Chop into small dices and put in a bowl with the rest of teh main ingredients, taste and adjust the seasoning.

Using a mould ¾ fill with the salmon dices and press down gently. Spoon on a layer of créme fraiche and smooth with a palette knife to get a clean finish.

Decorate around the top with small fonds of fresh dill. Place a circle of over lapping layers of cucumber in the centre of the serving plate bigger than your mould, place the mould onto the bed of salmon and lift off the leaving the salmon sitting on the cucumber.

Decorate the top with your chosen garnish and swizzle round the miso dressing.

Burgundy snails with chablis

1tin (850ml) of prepared
   snails – approx. 12 doz
   – strain and rinse in cold
   water
300g dried wild mixed
   mushrooms – soak in
   warm water for 30mins
   and chop roughly
1 quantity of puff pastry
3 shallots finely chopped
2tbsp white wine vinegar or
   tarragon vinegar
2 glasses white wine
sea salt and freshly ground
   black pepper
500ml crème fraîche
2tbsp flat leaf parsley/
   chervil chopped
3 cloves garlic, crushed with
   the back of a large knife
knob of butter
1tbsp olive oil
red baies

Pre-heat the oven to 220°C, 425°C.

Roll out the puff pastry and using a template 8cmx10cm, cut out 8 reasonably thick rectangles. Score an inner rectangle and score a lattice work carefully and gently across the smaller interior rectangle. Glaze with egg wash and bake in the oven until well risen and golden brown on top.

Cool on a wire rack and then carefully lift off the interior rectangle which is now the lid of your pastry parcels.

In a large sauté pan melt the butter and oil. Add the shallots and cook until soft. Add the snails and mushrooms – cook through for 10mins over medium heat.

Add the vinegar and reduce completely. Repeat this with the white wine but only reduce by half, then add the crème fraîche and garlic.

Stir well and leave to simmer for 15mins until the sauce starts to thicken. Stir through the chopped chervil or parsley just before serving. Season with salt and pepper.

To serve
Spoon over the puff pastry parcels and place the lids back on. Sprinkle with extra parsley/chervil and crushed red baies or omit the puff pastry stage and serve in a pretty pot with crunchy bread.

Hot smoked duck breasts

salt mix
180g sea salt flakes
180g light brown sugar
4tsp bruised black pepper
 corns
6 bruised fresh bay leaves
10 bruised juniper berries
4 fresh free range meaty
 duck fillets – skin on

Mix all the marinade ingredients together and rub generously over the duck fillets. Cover tightly with cling film and chill for several hours.

Rinse off the marinade and pat the duck dry – wrap in a clean tea towel and chill for at least 8hrs.

Prep the smoker according to manufacturer's instructions. Lay the duck breast on the rack and smoke for approx. 20mins – it should be still pink inside when you slice through.

If you want to eat them hot – *before* smoking slash the duck skin a couple of times and fry skin side down in a hot non stick frying pan (no extra fat should be added). Then smoke as above.

Leave to rest before eating for approx. 15mins or wrap and chill.

Delicious served diced in a salad mixed with a splash of hoi sin sauce.

Market
lunch

"Flavours and smells of a bustling market speak the universal language of joy, passion, life and love"

Scatty Chef

One of the joys of taking a group into the markets of France, England, Spain or any other quite frankly, (I've just been transported back to Marrakech and Goa for a second) the feeling is exactly the same. They are vibrant and full of hustle and bustle, the product of life coming from busy people haggling for the best deals, elbowing to get in line and heaving shopping bags stuffed full with the weekly shop.

As we wander back and forth through the wide alleys in Dijon, or even Barcelona, although the alleys are much closer together there, I get to see the enthusiasm and excitement through the eyes of people for some of which is their first experience of a European market. It reminds me just how lucky I am.

There is nothing nicer than purchasing something delicious and I always give 'carte blanche' for all my students to buy something that looks to good to eat. Perhaps something they have always wanted to try or that they have no idea exactly what it is, which can be highly amusing.

Embracing, even if it is just for a brief moment in time, the experience of local daily life is very satisfying and really makes people reflect their own routines.

As we sit in the main square, gazing up at the Ducal Palace constructed in the 14th century by Philip the Bold, enjoying a well earned cafe au lait or chocolat chaud, the discussion often turns to how they could adapt this style of shopping into their own lives.

I am a true believer that if one takes the time and trouble to source good seasonal ingredients from local producers then the rest will follow. Cooking will have more meaning and purposes, providing greater pleasure as you take pride in the dishes you have chosen to share with others.

Enjoying a market lunch out in the courtyard back at the Cookery School 'la ferme de la lochere', sat on top of the view point above Savigny le Beaune admiring the acres of vineyards splayed before you or sitting in a shady spot with friends on a summer afternoon is the epitome of 'French Life'.

No rush, no need to stress, just unwind and enjoy the simple pleasure of a market lunch.

SHOP. COOK. EAT.

Duck and pork rillettes

2kg pork belly
500g pork fat
4 duck legs
250ml white wine
6 sprigs of thyme
6 garlic cloves
6 whole star anise
10 fresh bay leaves
20 juniper berries lightly
** crushed**
4tsp salt
2tsp freshly ground black
** pepper**
2 blades of mace
3 cinnamon sticks
lard to seal

Put all the ingredients into a heavy bottomed saucepan except the lard and bring to a simmer.

Turn down the heat and cook very slowly with a lid on for at least 4 hours. Stir frequently to stop it sticking. The meat should be falling apart at this stage. Strain in a large colander over a big bowl and remove the herbs and mace.

Press down the meat to extract some of the fat. Shred the warm meat with two forks – I actually use my fingers, it's quicker and I just love the feel of it!

Put the meat and 100ml of strained juices into a clean pan and cook for 10mins, stirring all the time. Taste and season if needs be. Pack into dishes, and chill.

Alternatively, to keep longer use kilnar jars and heat seal for 40mins. If keeping in the fridge, melt a little lard and pour over the top of the dish to seal.

Serve with crackers, bread and a selection of pickles and chutneys.

Classic French crudités

2 cucumber, peeled, cut in
  half lengthways, deseed
  and sliced into slithers
300ml Greek yoghurt or
  fromage blanc
2 cloves garlic, peeled and
  smashed
small bunch of chives
salt and freshly ground
  black pepper
juice of 1 lemon

The cucumber salad
In a large bowl combine the Greek yoghurt or from age blanc
with the garlic, chopped chives, lemon juice, salt and pepper.
Add the sliced cucumber, stir well and chill for a good
30mins before serving.

If using the following day give it a good stir before serving
because the water from the cucumbers will be sitting on the
top of the yoghurt mix.

1 large celeriac, peeled and
  shredded
1 quantity of lemon
  mayonnaise with 2 extra
  spoons of Dijon mustard
  in it
small bunch of chervil

Celeriac salad
In a large bowl mix all the ingredients together and chill for
at least 30 mins. Check the seasoning before serving as it
might need a little more salt.

Sprinkle the chopped chervil over the creamy celeriac.

1.5kg of mixed heirloom
  tomatoes, washed and all
  cut into different slices,
  cubes or quarters
fresh basil
2 shallots, finely diced
salt and freshly ground
  pepper
good quality olive oil
thick white balsamic vinegar

For the heirloom tomato salad
Place all the tomatoes on a platter, drop the fresh basil over
them, season with salt and pepper, drizzle over the olive oil
and vinegar *or* any other flavoured oils you might have like
rocket or chive.

8 cooked, peeled and
  diced beets
Yannick's vinaigrette
  drizzled over (p.58)
chives cut into 4cm lengths
2 shallots finely diced

For the beetroot salad
Mix all ingredients together and serve chilled on a platter.

For the carrot salad
See the moroccan carrot salad, p.175.

Black olive and rosemary foccacia

1 **quantity of basic bread mix (see p.66) add to that a large handful of chopped black olives and 3 sprigs of rosemary roughly chopped**

topping
sun blushed tapenade (in a food processor add 200g sun blushed tomatoes, 2 tbsps olive oil, 3 cloves fresh garlic pinch of pepper and pureé until smooth)
3 shallots, finely chopped and softened in butter over a low heat
a mixture of confit mushrooms, drained from the oil (optional)
2 balls of mozzarella
sea salt and cracked pepper
fresh sprigs of rosemary

Roughly roll out your foccacia base into a rectangle and prod down with your fingers.

Spread over the tomato tapenade and then the shallots and mushroom.

Decorate with fresh rosemary, and torn off mozzarella pieces, Salt and pepper. Bake until well risen and the mozzarella is starting to turn golden brown.

Mackerel in Dijon mustard sauce

See page. 95

Black olives with extra virgin olive oil, garlic and parmesan

1kg Italian black olives
  Ponentine, Liguria,
  Lugano or Gaeta are
  delicious varieties
3 cloves of fresh garlic
2tbsp finely chopped basil,
  (be careful not to chop
  basil for too long or it will
  form a pureé
1tsp crushed black pepper
250ml delicious good
  quality virgin or cold
  press olive oil
200g roughly grated
  parmesan

In a large bowl mix all the ingredients together and marinade overnight.

To store for longer place the olives in an airtight jar and cover with some more olive oil to cover and secure with a lid. Store in a cupboard out of direct sunlight.

Country pâté for the pantry

See page. 99

Main
dishes

> "Cassoulet, like life itself, is not so simple as it seems."
>
> *Paula Wolfert*

It makes no difference to ones origins, there is something indisputably reminiscent about slow cooking that comes from our need to be nurtured and cosy in the winter months. The traditional French dishes of Cassoulet, Coq au Vin, Boeuf Bourguignon are infamous and the essence of traditional French farmhouse cuisine, but they can also be made to step up to a sophisticated supper party. It's one of my little tweaks that I love to share as often these masterful dishes go unused because they don't quite fit the bill for a fancy evening.

All you have to do is think outside the box!

The principal of good slow cooking is the quality of the meat you choice to cook with. When you find the right butcher, who is reliable and whom you trust, take him and nurture him and you will be blessed with the finest cuts therefore the most superb result. Do not compromise, and do not be palmed off with a lesser quality cut - time to look for a new butcher if this ever happens. If you have ever had the possibility to dine in a Michelin starred restaurants, you will no doubt have noticed that there was a rage a few years ago, in France anyway, where the classic dishes from the farm were deconstructed and presented in an entirely different way.

Let's take the King of Burgundy, Boeuf Bourguignon, a stew best cooked in a cast iron pot with lots of red wine and Charolais beef, hence the name, (Charolais is produced in Burgundy), slowly cooked for hours, usually the day before it is to be eaten.

The fat in the beef gives the sauce its flavour and the long cooking time makes it melt in the mouth. It's quite hard to make this dish look fancy and why should you? It's perfect just the way it is, but you can refine it if you want to, simply cutting the chunks of beef into more even sizes before cooking, taking the meat out of the pot and putting to one side once it's cooked, straining half the sauce off and reducing down with a spoon of redcurrant jelly and a knob of butter whisked to a shine. Turn the carrots and potatoes, cook separately and glaze in a small knob of butter. Place 2 pieces of meat per person in the center of the serving plate, spoon over some original sauce that will also have the onions, lardons and mushrooms in it.

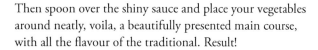

Then spoon over the shiny sauce and place your vegetables around neatly, voila, a beautifully presented main course, with all the flavour of the traditional. Result!

The same process can be applied for coq au vin, chicken Gaston Gerard, but with those I choose the same cut of meat as opposed to a whole chicken or cockerel, so every plate looks the same.

With fish, I always think less is best. So many people just fuss to much and usually end up disguising the delicate flavour that is the essence of fish with a creamy sauce, but it's just not necessary.

So lay off the fancy stuff and serve it with minimum fuss, elegant vegetables and a light sauce sparingly spooned around the fish. Sublime!

I've included sausages in the main courses, not because they necessarily need to be there, but I can't write the whole book about minced meats flavoured with spices, perhaps the next one! I love them, and to make metre after metre is such fun with new friends through my Cookery School or with my neighbours.

Bœuf bourguignon with beef cheeks

3 whole trimmed beef
cheeks cut into big
pieces. Approx. 4 people
per cheek or approx. 300g
per person of collar which
is delicious
a couple of bone marrow
chunks
500g little onions, peeled
and quartered or shallots
5 garlic cloves, peeled and
crushed
1tsp juniper berries
slightly smashed in a
pestle and mortar
2-3 cloves (optional)
400g smoked lardons or
smoky bacon rashers cut
into chunks
500g mushrooms, peeled if
necessary, thickly sliced
butter and oil for cooking
sea salt and freshly ground
black pepper
splash Cognac
2 bottles red wine
(Burgundy if you can)
500ml rich beef stock
6tbsp plain flour
handful of fresh thyme
5 fresh bay leaves
2tbsp chopped flat
leaf parsley

In a large pan big enough to put in the oven melt a little
butter and fry off the shallots/onions and bacon – set aside.
Mix the flour, salt and pepper together with the thyme and
meat. In the same pan, add some more butter and oil and
seal the meat. You will have to do this in batches so that it
doesn't start to stew rather than sizzle and colour the meat.

Don't worry if the pan sticks at the bottom, it will be fine
when the liquids are added. With all the meat sealed, set
aside the meat add Cognac – flambé. Scrape down the sides
and bottom of the pan to get all the meat juices and
caramelized bits off the bottom and into the sauce. Add
the red wine and beef stock. Return the beef to the pan
with the onion, shallots, bacon and garlic.

Throw in the cloves, juniper berries, bay leaves and bone
marrow if using any. Cover and leave to cook gently for
2-3hrs in a low oven.

Take out and taste. Cover and leave to rest overnight. Before
serving melt some butter in a pan and fry the mushrooms.
Add to the meat with half the chopped parsley. Return the
meat to the oven for 45mins.

Stir through the remaining chopped parsley before serving.

TIPS
Serve it simple with crunchy french bread and steamed
buttered potatoes

Turn your extractor fan off if you flambé - I speak from
experience as the flames went straight up the flu, burnt a hole in
the filter and was seen coming straight out of the top of the boat
I was working in front of the pilot!

Cassoulet french bean and pork hotpot

2kg dried white or the really
large fava haricot beans
soaked in cold water
for 12 hrs
2 boiling sausages
8 smoked toulouse sausages
600g salted pork belly
3 ½ salted (demi-sel) pork
knuckles
10 peeled carrots
10 peeled white onions
(medium)
10 cloves – stuck in a couple
of onions
11 fresh bay leaves, 8 large
sprigs of thyme, 4 large
sprigs of fresh rosemary
(tied together to for a
bouquet garni)
8 cloves of garlic smashed
15 black peppercorns and
the same of juniper
berries roughly smashed
in a pestle and mortar to
release the flavours
1.5kg shoulder of lamb cut
into 12 chunks
1.5kg tomatoes, peeled,
deseeded and diced
3tbsp chopped fresh flat
leaf parsley
6 preserved duck legs form
specialist shop or home
done
200g dried breadcrumbs
reserve a little of the duck
fat to brown the lamb
chunks

Drain and rinse the beans - Par cook in a large pan of salted
water with 3 bay leaves, a few juniper berries, lightly
smashed, salt and pepper - cook for 1hr and drain –
reserve until needed.

Fill a really large pan with cold water, prick the sausages and
add to the pan along with the rest of the pork meats. When
the water boils remove the sausages and refresh in cold water,
continue to cook the other meats for a further 6mins.

Drain and refresh and in a clean large saucepan, add the
carrots, onions, half the garlic, peppercorns, juniper berries
and bouquet garni. Bring to the boil and then reduce to a
simmer, skim every so often. After 30mins add the knuckle
and rind. After 1hr add the tomatoes and pork belly.

Heat up the goose fat in a frying pan and brown the lamb
pieces quickly, drain and set aside. After 1hr 45mins add the
lamb and boiling sausage to the stew. Add the beans.

After another 30mins quickly griddle the toulouse sausages
and add to the casserole, then add the duck legs. Continue
cooking for another 40mins. Season to taste.

Roll the remaining garlic in salt and place at the bottom
of the serving ovenproof pan.

Take out the pork rind and mince to a puree, add in the
parsley and breadcrumbs.

Spoon out the mixture into the ovenproof dish, slice and cut
the meat to place on top.

Add the breadcrumb mixture on top and bake for 45mins
to form a crust.

Serve piping hot with crusty French bread or foccacia

Confit of duck

12 duck legs
2 tbsp aromatic salt
1.5kg duck or goose fat
6 star anise
20 juniper berries
3 cinnamon sticks
20 crushed pepper corns

Rub aromatic salt over duck legs, cover and leave in fridge for 24 hours.

Melt fat in a large pan place legs in plus all the spices and simmer gently in oven for 3hrs or on the hob, but be careful the duck does not stick to the base of the pan.

Store in Kilner jars covered in fat and sterilize or if using immediately, drain off fat, place the duck legs on a rack and crisp up in a hot oven for 20mins or so.

Serve with a crispy green salad and hot potatoes or a delicious puree of parsnips. Or, shred and serve warm over roasted tomato salad.

Coq au vin

2 organic free range
   cockerels or mature
   chicken
4sp plain flour
15ml olive oil
40g butter
400g smoked lardons
2-3 chopped onions
6 carrots roughly chopped
2 medium leeks roughly
   chopped
handful of rosemary, thyme
   and fresh bay leaves
300ml Cognac
1 bottle of red wine maybe
   more!
500ml chicken stock
300g button mushrooms
4 sticks celery
3 cloves of garlic

Joint the coq or chicken and marinade in the red wine over night, take out strain, pat dry and reserve juice. You don't have to do this, but it might prove to add extra flavour.

Some recipes call for cooking the day before then reheating slowly the next before serving – I'm out on that one! – I guess it's time that might make the difference.

In a bowl put the flour, salt and pepper. Toss the meat in that. Lie on a plate and re-season.

Heat a large oven proof pan up and melt the butter and oil. Throw in the lardons and fry, add the chicken/coq and colour – this might take several batches if you have a lot of meat or a small pan. Spoon out and set aside.

Add all the vegetables and cook gently for 5mins, then add the Cognac and deglaze the pan. Add the wine and bring to a simmer.

Return the coq/chicken to the pan. Bring back to a simmer, taste and adjust the seasoning. Reduce the liquid by approximately ½. Add the stock. Taste again, season if necessary.

Cook uncovered until the liquid has reduced by half and the meat is soft and tender.

In a pan with a knob of butter and splash of oil, fry the mushrooms until golden.

Serve with vegetables and top with the mushrooms

Fish tagine with chorizo, spinach and pearl barley

12 cod fillets or another
    white fish less in danger
    like perhaps Pollack
300ml coconut milk
300ml cream
10 strands of saffron
zest of 2 lemons and 2 limes
3 star anise
1 cinnamon stick
5 crushed juniper berries
2 freshly made chorizo
    saucisson, not sausages,
    but the saucisson before it
    starts to dry out – cut on
    the diagonal into 1cm
    slices
4tsp freshly grated ginger
3 shallots finely diced
knob of butter
200g pearl barley
500ml vegetable stock
500g fresh young spinach
50ml white wine
smoked paprika
2 tbsp coriander oil – 5tbsp
    fresh coriander leaves
    blended with 4tbsp olive
    oil, pinch of salt and
    squeeze of lemon – sieved
    and kept in a plastic
    bottle with a nozzle

In a deep sauté pan or earthenware tagine dish, melt a knob of butter and sweat the shallots, do not colour them but they should be soft and translucent. Add the spices, lemon zest, ginger and saffron, then the wine.

Pour in the cream and milk stock then add the pearl barley, cover and cook for 20mins until the barley is soft and creamy.

In a sauté pan fry the chorizo until it starts to crisp up, remove and drain off the juice, but reserve it for later.

Slide the fish into the cream and cook gently for 6mins turning half way through. Then add the chorizo for 1min.

In a large pan wilt the spinach down and drain. Return to a pan with a knob of butter, and season with salt, pepper and a pinch of smoked paprika.

To serve
Spoon a tower of spinach into the centre of each shallow bowl and place a fillet of fish on top. Spoon round the sauce from the tagine making sure there are a few slices of chorizo on each plate. Swirl round a little reserved chorizo juice and coriander oil.

Duck breast with an infusion of Cointreau and orange

3 large duck breasts
2tsp fresh thyme
1tsp mixed spice
2tbsp orange zest plus
 the juice
juice of 2 limes
3tbsp Cognac
3tbsp Cointreau
30g chilled butter
sea salt and freshly ground
 black pepper

TIP
Don't be tempted to omit this
stage as the bitterness of
the orange zest will
be overwhelming and
ruin the sauce.

Preheat oven to 220°C, 425°F. Score the skins of the duck in parallel lines with a sharp knife, deeply enough to cut into the flesh.

In a small bowl, mix together the mixed spices, thyme, salt and pepper. Rub this into the flesh of the duck and into the cuts.

Heat a sauté pan until hot – place the duck breasts into the pan skin side down. Reduce the heat to moderate and cook for 5mins. If you feel that the skins are cooking too quickly, turn down the heat, but you are looking for them to become dark and slightly crunchy.

In the meantime, blanch the orange zests in boiling water for 2mins, drain and keep warm. Turn the duck breasts over and cook on a moderate heat for 2mins – take out and place on a baking tray covering them tightly in foil.

Keep the cooking pan on the stove as you will need it for the sauce, just turn off for now.

Transfer to the oven and cook for 5mins.

Remove, pour off the juice into a jug and keep the duck wrapped up to rest for 10mins warm.

Drain off a little of the fat from the pan (not down the sink as it will set when it is cold).

Turn up the heat and add the Cognac to the sauté pan – flambé – remember to turn off extractor fans before lighting! Add the orange and lime juice – simmer. Add the Cointreau and orange zest. Whisk in the butter and taste – adjust seasoning if necessary.

Open out the foil covering the duck and pour any meat juices into the pan. as well as the jug of already collected juices.

Slice the duck and place on a serving plate – the duck should be pink and utterly delicious.

Spoon over the sauce and serve immediately with a mirepoix
of vegetables and a slice of rosti potato.

Lamb shanks in tomatoes and red wine

8 lamb shanks
a pinch or 2 of some
   herbs de province
½ bottle of red wine
1ltr dark beef stock
2 medium onions, finely
   diced or 500g button
   onions
300g smoked pork belly
   (bacon) cut into chunks
   to make lardons approx.
   1cm cubes
knob of butter and olive oil
4 cloves smashed garlic
200g jar of redcurrant jelly
6 fresh bay leaves
6 sprigs of thyme
6 or so smashed juniper
   berries
freshly ground black pepper
   and coarse sea salt
8 peeled, deseeded and
   chopped tomatoes or a
   regular tin
30g or so of flour to coat the
   lamb shanks
½ glass Cognac to deglaze
   the pan and flambé
   (optional)

Preheat oven to 180°C, 350°F.

In a heavy cast iron pan suitable for the oven or a dish similar, the copper ones work well too, melt a knob of butter and add a splash of oil and heat to a sizzle.

Toss the shanks in the flour, season with salt and pepper and a few herbs de province, not too many as we are adding extra herbs later in the recipe. Brown the shanks all over and remove from the pan. Do this in batches or they will start to stew rather than brown deglaze the pan with the Cognac, watch your hands on the handle of the pan and remember my top tip!

Add another knob of butter and glug of oil and get it hot again. Pan fry the onions and lardons. Add all the liquids, tomatoes, herbs and spices (not the redcurrant jam yet) and bring to a simmer. The sauce should start to thicken slightly.

Return the shanks to the pot. Pop the lid on and put into the oven for 2 hours.

Take out and taste, stir through the redcurrant jelly, taste again. The jelly makes the sauce really shiny and removes the bitterness from the wine.

If you want to make the sauce thicker, remove a litre of sauce and reduce down in a pan by half stir. (You can also use a little flour and butter mixed together in a small bowl that you can then whisk into the sauce - it will dull the sauce slightly, so only use if it's really too runny)

TIPS
When you serve it, coat the shanks with the shiny glossy red sauce. Delicious!

Turn your extractor fan off if you flambé - I speak from experience as the flames went straight up the flu, burnt a hole in the filter and was seen coming straight out of the top of the boat I was working in front of the pilot!

Slow braised pork cheeks in rich ragout sauce

3kg trimmed pork cheeks,
*(you may well have to
order these cheeks from
your butcher, but persevere
as they truly are one of the
most delicious pieces of
meat that you will ever
taste and there is no fat
on them!)*
**500g or so of small white
baby onions, peeled**
500g smoked lardons
**3ltrs light meat stock, like
veal or light beef stock**
**2kg tomatoes, peeled
deseeded and chopped or
you can use canned, diced
tomatoes**
4 fresh bay leaves
**8 sprigs fresh thyme, pulled
of the sprigs**
60g flour
50ml Cognac
250ml red wine
**5 garlic cloves, peeled and
crushed**
**1tsp juniper berries and 2-3
cloves (optional)**
butter and oil for cooking
salt and pepper

Pre heat oven to 170°C, 325°F. In a large bowl, put the flour, a good grind of salt and black pepper. Toss the pork cheeks in the flour.

Heat up a large oven proof casserole dish until hot, then add a knob of butter and a splash of oil. Fy off the onions and lardons until slightly colured then set aside. Seal the pork cheeks in batches until just coloured. Add more butter and oil if the meat sticks too much.

Deglaze the pan with a good splash of Cognac and flambé. *Remember - you know what can happen!* Scrape all the good bits off the bottom of the pan and stir until the Cognac has almost evaporated. Pour in the red wine, still stirring and half the stock then the tomatoes.

Return all the meats and onions to the pan. Bring to a simmer and add the bay leaves and thyme. Cover the pan and cook gently in a moderate oven for 1h 30mins then check to see how tender the meat is and how thick the sauce is. Add more stock if necessary, adjust the seasoning at this stage too.

Return to the oven probably for another hour. Check again for tenderness of meat. It should just melt in the mouth. Once cooked drain off ¾ of the sauce. Blend until smooth and pour into a saucepan. Reduce down by a half. Add 2 tablespoons of redcurrant jelly to give the sauce a shiny coating, whisk thoroughly and taste.

Arrange the meat on a serving plate with the onions and lardons and spoon over the reduced sauce to finish.

Serve with glazed carrots, parsnip dauphinoise or buttered spinach.

Slow braised pork belly with home-made pesto

5kg length of pork belly
large bowl full of fresh herbs
  tarragon, flat leaved
  parsley, thyme, marjoram,
  chervil, sage, hyssop,
  lemon thyme, lemon balm
  etc *or* any fresh green
  herbs in season
3tbsp sea salt
1tbsp coarsely ground
  pepper
1tbsp aromatic spice mix
butchers string
20 fresh bay leaves
3tbsp fresh home made
  pesto
8 medium onions
1ltr apple juice, cider,
  Cognac, white wine or
  just water
large roasting tin

Preheat oven to 100°C, 200°F. With a sharp knife, take the skin off the pork belly and keep for crackling. Turn the pork belly over and cut off the ribs (use to lay in the bottom of the roasting tin and place rolled pork belly on top during cooking). Roughly chop the fresh herbs.

Mix 1tbsp sea salt and coarsely ground pepper together with the aromatic spice mix and rub generously all over the pork both sides.

On the rib side spread over the pesto and the roughly chop the herbs. Roll the pork tightly, lengthways and secure with butchers string every 4cm.

Cut the onions into halves leaving the skin on. Place the meat in the bottom of the roasting pan, on the ribs that were cut off earlier, add the onions and all the bay leaves. Half fill the pan with apple juice, cider, Cognac or white wine.

Fill the roasting pan to halfway with water and cover very tightly with foil. Place in the oven on the minimum heat for 12hrs. Take out and wrap the meat in foil and cool until it can be put in the fridge. Leave overnight then take out, cut into steak sized pieces. Pan fry in a good non stick pan until caramelized on both sided. Transfer to an oven dish, cover with foil and keep warm in the oven until needed.

Peel the skin off the onions and blend the onions with the cooking juices to form an onion sauce.

Serve with pan fried buttered apples flambéed with Cognac or with creamy butter beans.

Smoked haddock and cod with green asparagus, pea coulis

one fillet portion per person of both smoked haddock, the dyed type and cod

30 green young asparagus, peeled and trimmed to 8cm

splash of mandarin oil

pea coulis

300g petit pois fresh or frozen

1 shallot, peeled and finely chopped

1tsp butter

200ml hot veg or chicken stock

50ml cream

pinch of sea salt and ground black pepper

1tbsp fresh mint leaves

plastic squeezy bottle (if you don't have one use a small teaspoon)

Preheat oven to 220°C, 425°F.

Bring a large pan of salt water to a boil. Plunge the green asparagus in and cook for 2mins. Drain and immediately transfer into ice cold water for a further 5mins to keep them green. Drain and pat dry.

Lay a large sheet of foil on the first baking tray, brush lightly with oil and lay the pieces of cod on it - season sparingly with salt and pepper, cover with 2nd sheet of foil and fold the edges together to form a tight seal all the way round.

Repeat on the 2nd baking tray with the haddock, but do not season with salt! Cook the haddock for no more than 5mins and the cod for 8-10mins depending on its thickness, less rather than more.

In a small pan sweat shallots in the teaspoon of butter until transparent. Pour in the peas and veg stock, cook for 1min. Blend with the mint leaves and seasoning until smooth.

Sieve and stir in the cream, it should not be completely liquid but like a coating sauce. Pour into a plastic squeezy bottle.

To serve
On a serving dish of your choice lay out 5 asparagus in the middle of the plate place a piece of cod on a slant on top of the ends of the asparagus and place the haddock on an opposite slant on top of the cod. Brush the haddock with a thin film of oil to make it shiny.

Decorate the plate with the petit pois coulis either in swirls or dots. Serve immediately.

Chicken 'Gaston Gérard'

2 whole free-range chickens, chopped into pieces or 12 breasts with skin or legs, or whatever cut you prefer!
sea salt, smoked paprika and freshly ground black pepper
100g butter
3 bay leaves
10 sprigs of flowering thyme
splash of Cognac
splash of tarragon or white wine vinegar
500ml cream or crème fraiche
½ bottle of dry white burgundy wine
50g dijon mustard
300ml chicken stock
200g grated Gruyere or Beaufort

In a mixing bowl and season the chicken pieces with the salt, pepper and paprika.

Melt the butter in a sauté pan and colour all the chicken pieces. Add the bay leaves and thyme and cover.

Cook for approx. 10mins turning the chicken half way through. Transfer the chicken pieces to an earthenware pot or other ovenproof dish with a lid.

Preheat oven to 200°C, 400°F.

Deglaze the pan with Cognac, flambé. Then add the white wine vinegar, reduce to nothing then add the white wine and reduce by half.

Add the cream or crème fraîche, mustard and chicken stock and half the cheese, stir until smooth and pour over chicken. Cover and cook in the oven for 20mins.

Take off lid and turn on grill.

Serve with, potato dauphinoise and girolles mushrooms or haricot blanc and ribbon leeks

Easy smoked style sausage

2kg smoked pork shoulder, cut into cubes
500g fatty pork belly, cut into cubes
40g salt
35g sugar
20g toasted fennel seeds
6g cracked black pepper
4g ground nutmeg
1 cup minced fresh parsley
1 head garlic, peeled and chopped
300ml dry sherry
120ml sherry vinegar

Grind your meats, starting with the coarse disc on the grinder and reducing afterwards to the finer one, if you wish– chill.

Warm the fennel in a clean non stick frying pan to release the flavours then grind. Mix the fennel, salt, sugar and pepper into the meats.

Combine the sherry vinegar with the sherry or Madeira. Soak approx. 10m of sausages casing in warm water. Then run warm water through it to see if there are any holes, obviously this should be done over the sink! Thread the casing onto the sausage stuffer attachment of the grinder.

Mix the liquids to the meat.

Do not tie a knot in the end of the sausage casing as the air is the first thing out of the grinder not the meat. It takes some practice but it is relatively easy to then produce your sausages by feeding the meat in the top of the grinder and then it gently appearing out the sausage attachment into the casing. Tie the ends of the casing securely once all the ground meat is through the grinder.

Hang the sausages up if possible and with a sterilized needle look for air bubbles and prick sharply and the air should escape. Dry them for a few hours or overnight and then freeze for later use or cook.

Merguez sausages

1.5kg diced beef or lamb
400g diced fatty pork belly
  or fatty lamb belly
10 cloves garlic, skinned and
  smashed
6 tbsp chopped fresh
  coriander
2 tbsp moroccan merguez
  spice mix (see p.54)
3-5tsp harissa

Grind the meats, mix with the remaining ingredients and
leave to rest for a few hours in the fridge.

Combine all ingredients in a large bowl, kneading the
mixture well to evenly distribute the spices, herbs and harissa.

Using a sausage maker stuff into the sausage casings.

To let the flavour mature, leave the merguez to mature for
a few days before eating.

Suitable for freezing.

Toulouse herb sausages with garlic

2kg shoulder of pork, cubed
1kg fatty pork belly, cubed
50g salt
1.5tsp ground black pepper
2tbs chopped fresh parsley
  or a mixture of herbs
3 garlic cloves crushed
½ freshly ground nutmeg

Put all the ingredients in a big bowl and mix with your hands
until the herbs are evenly distributed.

Before stuffing the skins, leave the meat to marinade for
a few hours in the fridge. Make up the sausages using the
same method as for 'Easy Smoked Sausages' *(above)*.

Cook within a few days or freeze.

SHOP. COOK. EAT.

Home made white pudding 'Boudin Blanc' with fresh herbs

350g brioche made into crumbs
250ml milk
2 cloves
7 shallots, finely chopped
65g butter
600g turkey breast
450g pork belly – no rind
8 free range eggs
500ml double cream
60ml white port or sherry
1tbsp cornflour
25g fine salt
20g truffles, finely chopped or 1tsp truffle juice which can be found in some specialist shops. *This* **is optional and some lovely fresh chopped herbs like chervil or coriander are just as nice**
100g clarified butter
1tbsp olive oil
10 metres sausage casing
60g coarse sea salt
2ltrs of milk

Bring the milk to a simmer with 2 cloves, add the brioche crumbs to the milk and leave to infuse. Soften a knob of butter and sweat the shallots until transparent, chill.

Cut the meats into cubes and grind in a mincer or blender, chill. Whisk the eggs together with the cream and the incorporate slowly into the meats. Add the brioche mix.

In a small bowl, mix together the port, cornflour, shallots and salt then add to the meats together with the truffles or the fresh herbs. If you have an electric sausages maker great! If not, use a funnel and stuff the casing with the meat mixture, you will need an assistant for this!

Tie every 10cm with string to make your boudins or fold in half, twist the fold again, twist, fold again then twist, just like the pro's!

In a large pan pour in 2ltrs of milk and 2ltrs of water plus a large handful of the coarse sea salt. Immerse the boudin and watch carefully – do not let it even begin to simmer but let it poach gently for 15mins then take off the stove and very gently lift out onto a clingfilm wrapped roasting tray. Cover with clingfilm and when cool chill overnight in the fridge.

To cook the boudin – lightly score the casing and lift the boudin out without breaking it. Roll the boudin in melted clarified butter and fry gently in a sauté pan until lightly golden all over, or cook in the oven.

Serve with creamy mashed potatoes with added chopped truffle and apple compote with Cognac.

TIP
Start with a coarse grinder attachment and then change to a fine one as the pork fat will get tangled up in the fine one and put you off for life from this recipe!

Salads

The preparation of good food is merely another expression of art, one of the joys of civilized living."

Dione Lucas

It's astonishing that the word 'salad' can mean *so* many different things.

To some it's just some green leaves on a plate with a bottle of shop bought dressing.

For others it is a 'melange' of crispy juicy young leaves from a variety of plants dressed with virgin cold pressed olive oil, a twist of lemon and a sprinkle of flaked smoked sea salt. A chilled sardine and bulgar wheat salad doesn't even contain lettuce, likewise the sweet spiced Moroccan carrot salad or the Jewelled Tabbouleh.

Delicious variations, endless combinations from all over the world, cold salads, warm salads, leafy salads, meaty salads, it's never ending. It is all delightful to the eye, fragrant to the nose and wonderfully tasty.

I am passionate about the art of a good salad.

I think that one thing is for sure; you have to trust your food compatibility gene. Believe in your senses to know that kiwi and blueberries work well on a green salad drizzled with raspberry vinegar and dotted with blue cheese, even if you've never had it before. Trust your eye for colour as I find that attention to colour is a good gauge to getting the flavours right.

I make salads all year round; in the winter it's a roasted beets, and goat's cheese with roasted cherry tomatoes or roasted sweet potatoes with bacon bits and walnuts. In the summer just about anything really! I love the soft skins of the first courgettes shredded into ribbons and served with fresh dill fronds and viola flowers all from the garden, or heirloom tomatoes simply with olive oil and lemon juice sprinkled with cinnamon basil and swirls of rocket oil with a pinch of salt.

Get creative, trust your instincts and you won't go wrong!

Sweet Moroccan carrot salad

6 large fresh carrots
(preferably just dug – this does not mean jumping over the fence to your neighbours veggie patch!), **peeled and shredded on a mandolin or in a food processor if you have to – on the mandolin the flavour of the carrots is stronger as the food processor extracts more liquid**
2tbsp mixed seeds – courgette, pumpkin, linseed etc.
3tbsp runny honey – local please – lavender is a very good choice
2tbsp olive oil
3tbsp chopped fresh mint
3tbsp orange concentrate

Blanch the carrots for 2mins in salted boiling water if using mandolin.

Mix all the other ingredients, except the fresh mint and seeds, together in a bowl.

Add the carrots and chill for 30mins.

Add the seeds and mint then chill again for at least 30mins.

Serve with a deliciously warm tart or as a starter with other Moroccan salads and fresh pitta or naan bread with hummus.

Fragrant jewelled green tabbouleh

500g couscous,
1 cucumber, skinned,
deseeded and diced finely
3 green peppers, deseeded
and diced finely
3 limes, zest, segments
and juice
juice of 2 lemons
3tbsp toasted flaked
almonds
olive oil, good quality
1 large onion, finely diced
and softened in a knob of
butter
1pkt lardons cooked with
the onions
1 large bunch mint roughly
chopped at the last
minute
1 bunch coriander
1 handful of red cranberries
and or the seeds of 2
pomegranates
salt and pepper
1 heaped tbsp curry spices
– raz el hanout and
aromatic salt (see p.57)

Measure out 500g couscous and place in a large bowl with a splash of olive oil and the spices, salt and pepper.

Run your fingers through the couscous to coat evenly with olive oil, as this will help prevent sticking.

Pour over 450ml boiling water and fork through the couscous gently and quickly – *Do not* over stir or it will stick. Cover and leave for 5mins.

Uncover and fork quickly through adding more olive oil to stop it sticking.

Add all the other ingredients, season and chill.

Before serving, taste and adjust the seasoning.

Sardines or mackerel stuffed with currants, pistachios and bulgar wheat

stuffing
80g bulgar wheat
handful of currants or
  sultanas
small handful of toasted
  pistachios toast in a frying
  pan or in the oven)
zest of 1 lemon
handful of chervil, chopped
  finely
pinch of cinnamon
generous handful of fresh
  mint, finely chopped
1 garlic clove, crushed
generous pinch of aromatic
  salt
80ml olive oil
2 preserved lemons,
  chopped finely

for the fish
10 sardine fillets
splash of olive oil
2 lemons
pinch of sugar
sea salt and freshly ground
  black pepper

Preheat oven to Gas 5, 200°C

Soak the wheat in a bowl of warm water and leave for 30mins. Drain and set aside.

Mix all the ingredients together in a bowl.

Toss the fish in the olive oil, sugar, salt and pepper.

Stuff the fish with a spoonful of filling and secure with a cocktail stick.

Place in a baking dish and cook for 5mins.

Serve warm with lemon wedges on a bed of salad or rocket.

Roasted chickpeas with sun blushed tomatoes and rosemary

500g cooked chickpeas

5 cloves garlic, smashed with the back of a heavy knife

2tbsp olive oil

knob of butter

3 large sprigs of rosemary, stripped

2tsp flaked smoked salt

2tsp crushed black pepper corns

200g sun blushed tomatoes

2tsp cummin seeds

1tsp ground cardomon

Roast in a medium 200-220°C oven, covered with foil for 1hr then remove foil and continue to roast until golden brown.

If you prefer the chickpeas to be soft, keep the foil on, but crunchy, nutty chickpeas are delicious!

Serve with Girolle and Halloumi Tart, Sweet Morrocan Carrot Salad and a fresh leafy wild rocket and spinach salad.

French bean salad with orange dressing and zest

500g french beans blanch for 3mins, drain and plunge into cold water to preserve the colour

1 quantity of orange dressing (see p.52)

1 orange, zested using a vegetable peeler and slicing into julienne, blanch and refresh twice

1tbsp walnut oil

large chopped bunch of chives

a handful of blanched fresh garden peas, when in season

Mix all the ingredients together and chill before serving.

Sweet potato roasted with maple syrup, crunchy lardons and pecans

1kg sweet potatoes, left
  unpeeled and cut into
  chunks
2 large onions, peeled and
  cut into thick chunks
generous splash of olive oil
a good handful of aromatic
  salt mix (see p.57)
freshly ground black pepper
a large handful of fresh
  chopped coriander, flat
  leaf parsley, chervil and
  salad onion
50g pecans or walnuts,
  toasted and chopped
50g golden sultanas
300g panfried lardons,
  cooked until crunchy

dressing
100ml olive oil
50ml maple syrup
30g xérès vinegar
juice of 2 lemons
juice and zest of 3 oranges
6 cm chunk of fresh ginger,
  peeled and grated
½tsp ground fennel seeds

Preheat the oven to 200°C.

Toss the potatoes and onion with the olive oil, pepper and aromatic salt. Roast until a knife inserted goes in easily, turn a couple of times during cooking. Approx. 40mins.

In a bowl whisk together all the dressing ingredients.

Tip the potatoes and onions into a serving bowl, tip in the herbs and toss together with the sultanas and nuts. Sprinkle throw the crunchy lardons.

Pour oven dressing and serve whilst still warm.

Variegated aubergine with green tahini and coriander marinade

1 white, 1 stripey, 1 purple
   aubergine
a splash of olive oil
freshly ground pepper and
sea salt to taste

marinade
1 red chilli, seeds removed
   and finely chopped
3tbsp chopped coriander
3tbsp chopped marjoram/
   oregano or flat leaf parsley
juice of 2 lemons
2 garlic cloves, peeled and
   crushed
100ml olive oil
large pinch sea salt or
   aromatic salt
freshly ground black pepper

green tahini
equal amounts of tahini
   paste and water approx.
   120ml of each
2 large garlic cloves or 3
   small ones, peeled and
   crushed
a good pinch of sea salt
50g flat leaved parsley or
   coriander or a mix of both
   – chop finely

Preheat oven to 200°C Gas 6.

Cut the aubergines in half lengthways, then again and then into quarters to form wedges.

In a bowl drizzle in a glug of olive oil and sprinkle on a good pinch of salt and pepper.

Heat up a griddle pan if you have one. Toss the aubergines in the oil and griddle to colour, transfer to an oven tray and roast for 25mins until soft inside.

Make the marinade. Mix all the ingredients in a bowl.

When the aubergines are ready spoon over the marinade and leave to absorb for a couple of hours.

For the tahini sauce
Blend everything in a blender except for the herbs, until smooth, adding more water if it is too thick.

Stir through the herbs and chill until needed.

Before serving decorate with some herbs and spoon over the green tahini dressing.

Figs, buffalo mozzarella, sun-blushed tomatoes and basil salad with roast garlic and fig dressing

mixed washed freshly picked
salad leaves including
peppery organic wild
rocket if you can find it-it
adds a real kick!
radicchio, frisee, mache,
Batavia etc
3 delicious lumps of the best
buffalo mozzarella you
can afford or find
8 plump black, rip figs with
a wonderful ruby interior,
cut into halves
20 sun blushed tomato
halves
a generous handful of fresh
basil leaves
freshly ground black pepper
and coarse sea salt

In a large rustic salad bowl arrange the salad leaves.

Tear the mozzarella into rough pieces and dot over the salad leaves, then arrange the sun blushed tomatoes, fig halves and basil leaves.

Sprinkle over the sea salt and pepper then drizzle over the roast garlic and fig dressing.

Use as much roast garlic and fig dressing as you like!

Beetroot, tomato and cured ham salad with orange dressing

1kg beetroots, cooked or
roasted
2 shallots or 1 small onion
large bowl of washed rocket
1 bunch chervil
1 quantity of orange
dressing (see p.52)
8 thin slices of cured ham
20 cherry tomatoes or
a variety of assorted
colours, shapes and sizes

Place the rocket on a large shallow salad bowl or platter. Cut the beetroots into chunky wedges, do the same to the tomatoes. Arrange the beetroots and tomatoes over the rocket.

Finely chop the shallots and sprinkle over salad. Arrange cured ham in swirls over salad.

Drizzle over the vinaigrette and decorate with willowy swathes of chervil.

Peppery leaf salad with lemon scented dressing

**a selection of young
colourful salad leaves
from the market, washed
and spun**
a selection of fresh herbs
lemon dressing (see p.51)
**Greek yoghurt or half
fromage blanc and
crème frais**
1 lemon plus zest
2tbsp grapeseed oil
3tsp lemon oil
**1tbsp tarragon wine vinegar
or fruity vinegar such as
raspberry or blackberry**
salt and pepper

In a large bowl mix all the ingredients together, taste and
adjust the seasoning.

Other herbs can also be added to this dressing or a teaspoon
of Dijon Mustard with different flavours can be added.

Tomato and basil salad with fresh goats cheese

**1.5-2kg tomatoes in several
different colour or
varieties, if possible**
**A selection of sun blushed
tomatoes in different
colours**
1 bunch basil
**2 fresh goats cheeses
(approx. 50g each) or
buffalo mozzarella or feta**
**4tbsp extra virgin olive oil
or extra virgin sunflower oil**
2tbsp balsamic vinegar
**freshly ground salt and
pepper**
1tsp dijon mustard
3tsp honey
2 shallots or fresh garlic

Core and finely slice the tomatoes. Arrange on a serving
platter. Tear chunks of the fresh goats cheese and dot over the
tomatoes.

In a bowl mix together with a small whisk the mustard and
oil. Slowly whisk in the vinegar, then season with salt and
pepper, the shallot, garlic and honey.

Drizzle over the tomatoes and goats cheese and decorate with
fresh basil leaves.

Chill before serving.

Salad niçoise - *the way I like it!*

800g responsibly sourced
   fresh tuna
olive oil, for rubbing on
   the tuna
sea salt and freshly ground
   black pepper
20 anchovy fillets (not the
   ones packed in salt)
700g green beans, trimmed
   and blanched so they still
   have a crunch
700g yellow beans, trimmed
   and blanched so they still
   have a crunch
1kg salad (rattes) potatoes,
   scrubbed, cooked with
   their skins. They need to
   remain firm
1 red and 1 yellow pepper,
   thinly sliced
10 different funky tomatoes,
   hopefully from the
garden, washed, stem
   removed and cut into bit
   sized pieces
8 free range eggs, soft
   cooked, peeled and cut
   in half
100g delicious olives (they
   don't have to be niçoise
   olives, just delicious)
chervil to garnish

for the dressing
12 tablespoons olive oil
6 tablespoons red wine
   vinegar
1tsp Dijon mustard
generous grind of fresh
   black pepper
3 cloves garlic, pressed
8 anchovy fillets, chopped
   fine

For the dressing
Blitz the whole lot in a mood processor and store in a jar in
the fridge until needed. Give it a good shake to loosen it up
before pouring over.

And the rest
If you have a griddle, heat it up until smoking. Lay a few
strips of rosemary on, rub the tuna with a little olive oil and
set on the grill covering the rosemary.

Cook for approx. 7mins turning half way through, remove
and cover. Leave to rest at room temperature.
Drain the anchovies of oil.

Pick a lovely oval platter if you have one and pile up with the
beans and peppers. Arrange the potatoes, tomatoes, soft
cooked eggs and anchovies over the top. Drizzle over some
anchovy dressing.

Break the tuna apart into large pieces and arrange on top.
Pop the olives on, drizzle over some more anchovy dressing.
Decorate with chervil.

It's summer on a plate! Yum.

TIP
*If it is still too thick add a little water and shake, keep adding
until it is a pouring consistency*

Tarts
Savoury

> *"You don't have to cook fancy or complicated masterpieces – just good food from fresh ingredients."*
>
> *Julia Child*

There is nothing more satisfying than watching a freshly made quiche cooking, all puffed up with a slightly cracked surface allowing the filling to peak through, especially, if you have used free-range eggs which are usually bright yellow. My preference is to eat them hot, as to present it just after it has been removed from the oven is far more impressive that making it and serving it the next day. It is still delicious of course but it's just that first view that's unbeatable.

A crispy flavoursome crust with some aromatic spices in it, is vital to achieving the perfect result. If the crust is substandard you can fill it full off the most delicious ingredients but there will still be something missing.

Savoury tarts, tortes and 'en croute' recipes are the perfect excuse to use the pastry as a vessel to pack in as much deliciousness as possible, liberally sprinkled with fresh herbs and held together with fresh deep yellow farm eggs and crème fraîche or cream, it's difficult to beat for flavour.

I am particularly fond of the classic quiche Lorraine, as it was one the very first dishes I made at school. Back then in the 'old days' as my children love to say, I was taught to make my pastry with half butter half lard. Can you imagine the horror if we did this today! We'd probably be arrested by the food police. But it surely makes a crispy crust! Well worth the risk in my humble opinion. I love a really deep crust as it allows even more smoked lardons and caramelized onions to be used, held together with cream and eggs. So good!

Tarts and pies from many countries are steeped in tradition from Pastys, pâte en croute, samosas, Jamaica patties, pork pies, pirozhiki, spanakopita, the list is endless.

All totally delicious with many originally designed to be carried and enjoyed by workers toiling hard in manual jobs. Using ingredients that were grown on the smallholding, preserved meats, everything can be cooked in a savoury tart. Quite often along with Frittata, omelettes and risotto, using vegetables, bacon, salmon or other items left in the fridge that just isn't quite enough to make a main meal can be made into something delicious once mixed with eggs and cream, baked until golden and puffed enjoyed with a crisp salad or warm potatoes. So simple!

Smoked salmon sunflower pie with goats cheese

400g puff pastry (see p.70)
_or_ order like I do from the
baker the week before if I
am too busy to make it)
8 slices of smoked salmon or
fresh salmon cooked or
any other fish for that
matter, haddock is fab too
100g soft white goats cheese
and mozzarella
sea salt and freshly ground
black pepper
½ lemon (juice and zest)
2 tbsp crème fraîche
2 tbsp fresh dill, chopped
egg wash

Preheat oven to 220°C, 400°F.

Divide puff pastry into 2 even sizes.

Roll out to make 2 squares the same size that will fit on
a baking tray and in your oven.

Cover baking tray with greasproof paper/baking parchment
and lie one pasty square on top.

In the middle of the square score very lightly a circle approx.
12cm in diameter.

Dot a third of the goats cheese and mozzarella in the middle,
then cover with half the smoked salmon and a spoon of
crème fraîche, give it a squeeze of lemon, sprinkle over some
of the lemon zest, some of the dill, salt and pepper.

Repeat once more finishing with final layer of cheese,
mozzarella, dill, squeeze of lemon, zest, salt and pepper.

With a pastry brush egg wash the pastry base and
carefully place the 2nd pastry square over the 1st one.
Press down firmly.

With a sharp small knive carefully cut leaves all around the
salmon and cheese mound – do not cut right up to the
mound – leave approx. 1.5cm border.

Score the petals with the knife gently and then quicky
jab little all over the salmon and cheese mound to form
the seeds.

Brush with egg wash and sprinkle over some sea salt.
Bake until golden and risen.

Deep fill provençal tart

300g plain flour
185g butter
1 free range egg
1tsp coarse ground sea salt
a dash of milk
or see p.71
throw in 1tsp of herbs de provence in the mix or a 1tsp of fresh thyme

filling
1tbsp olive oil and a little more maybe!
3 medium onions, peeled and sliced
3 red peppers, deseeded and chopped into slices
3 green peppers, deseeded and chopped into slices
2 courgettes/zucchini cut into 1.5cm cubes
1 aubergine/egg plant cut into 3cm slices
25 small cherry tomatoes
6 cloves of garlic peeled and smashed to a pulp
small bunch of tarragon
small bunch of basil
Dijon mustard for the base, or you can use pesto or a rich confit tomato paste
6 eggs
400ml cream or 300ml cream and 100ml milk. *You can replace the cream with crème fraîche. You can also use a garlic cream cheese which is delicious!*
salt
pepper
herbs de provence

Mix all the ingredients up in a food processor apart from the egg and milk. When it resembles breadcrumbs stop the machine, crack in the egg and the splash of milk. Blend again until it forms a ball of dough – chill for 30mins-1hr.
or
Make by hand – chill for 30mins-1hr.

Take out of fridge and on a lightly floured board roll out your pastry to fit the tart case (loose bottom tins are great if you can find them).

Be firm when you line it and don't worry about the cracks, dip your finger in a little cold water and dab it on the crack and either patch with extra pastry or push the two edges back together. Prick the base with a fork.

Chill until needed and leave the edges hanging over the top of the tart case.

Preheat the oven to 200°C, 400°F. Line the base with baking parchment and weigh down with baking beans. Cook the case blind for 35mins remove the paper and beans 15mins before the end and trim the pastry.

Toss the cherry tomatoes in a splash of olive oil and place in a roasting pan, tear off some basil, place with the tomatoes, season with salt and pepper and a few cloves of the garlic. Roast until they are coloured remove and drain off sauce – set aside until needed. Repeat for the aubergines and for the courgettes, but use tarragon. Roast both vegetables separately.

In a frying pan, heat up a glug of the olive oil. Fry off the onions and peppers until they start to caramelise. Set aside all the vegetables until they are cool.

Put the eggs, cream, milk, salt and pepper and herbs in a bowl and stir together.

Spread the Dijon mustard over the pre cooked pastry base. Spoon in the onions followed by the rest of the vegetables and some leaves of fresh tarragon, pour over the cream and egg mixture.

Cook in the oven for 30-40mins until risen and coloured.

Super rich quiche lorraine

300g plain flour
185g butter
1 free range egg
1tsp coarse ground sea salt
a dash of milk
or see p.71
throw in 1tsp of herbs de
   provence in the mix or a
   1tsp of fresh thyme

filling
1tbsp olive oil
3 medium onions, peeled
   and chopped
400g smoked rindless bacon
   cut into lardons
250g grated cheddar,
   medium strength or full
   flavoured
Dijon mustard for the base,
   or you can use pesto or a
   rich confit tomato paste
5 eggs
400ml cream or 300ml
   cream and 100ml milk.
   You can replace the cream
   with crème fraîche. You
   can also use a garlic cream
   cheese which is delicious!
salt
pepper
herbs de provence

Mix all the ingredients up in a food processor apart from the egg and milk. When it resembles breadcrumbs stop the machine, crack in the egg and the splash of milk. Blend again until it forms a ball of dough - Chill for 30mins-1hr.
or
Make by hand - chill for 30mins-1hr.

Take out of fridge and on a lightly floured board roll out your pastry to fit the tart case (loose bottom tins are great if you can find them). Be firm when you line it and don't worry about the cracks, dip your finger in a little cold water and dab it on the crack and either patch with extra pastry or push the two edges back together.

Prick the base with a fork. Chill until needed and leave the edges hanging over the top of the tart case.

Preheat oven to 200°C, 400°F.

In a frying pan, add olive oil and fry onions until transparent, add the lardons. Cook for 5 mins until all the excess liquid has evaporated and they start to caramelize. Set aside to cool.

Put the eggs, cream, milk, salt & pepper and herbs in a bowl and stir together.

Spread the Dijon mustard over the base. Spoon in the onions and lardons, cover with the cheese and pour over the cream and egg mixture.

Trim the sides of the pastry and cook in the oven for 30-40 mins until risen and coloured.

Savoury pumpkin and bacon pie

One quantity of shortcrust
pastry (see p.71)
a generous handful of dried
   herbs or spices
1kg mixture of peeled
   pumpkin wedges
500g other squashes, peeled
   and cut into wedges
4 shallots, peeled and sliced
   long ways into wedges
2tsp aromatic salt
splash of olive oil
salt and freshly ground
   black pepper
5 eggs
400g crème fraîche
salt and freshly ground
black pepper
3tsp Dijon mustard
30g green olives, de-stoned
   and roughly chopped
30g preserved garlic,
   roughly chopped
150g bacon bits, fried and
   drained to remove excess
   fat

to finish
60g toasted and chopped
   pecan nuts
chopped chives
¼ red chilli, deseeded and
finely chopped

Add the herbs or spices to the shortcrust pastry and chill. Line a quiche tin, chill until needed.

Preheat oven to 230°C. Toss the pumpkin pieces, shallots and aromatic salt and pepper in the olive oil.

Spread out over on a large baking tray and roast for 35mins.

Preheat oven to 220°C.

Prick the base of the pastry case with a fork, spread the olives, garlic and mustard over the base.

Fill the pie with the pumpkin and other squashes, sprinkle over the bacon bits.

In a big jug mix the eggs and crème fraîche together with the salt and pepper.

Carefully pour over the pie and bake in the pre heated oven for 30-40mins depending on the size of the tart case.

When the tart is cooked remove and take out of the tart case.

Sprinkle over the chopped nuts, chilli and chives.

Serve with a green salad and a simple french vinaigrette or a warm roasted tomato salad.

Potato and coriander pie

600g shortcrust pastry
1.5kg cooked potatoes,
    peeled and thinly sliced
3 cloves garlic, crushed
450ml crème fraîche
4 eggs
30g butter
3 tbsp fresh coriander,
    chopped
sea salt and freshly ground
    pepper

Preheat oven to 200°C, 400°F.

Roll out the pastry and line a deep spring tin cake or pie tin approx. 20cm in diameter – leave the pastry hanging over the edge of the tin to trim off once the lid has been put on.

In layers fill the pastry shell with potatoes seasoning as you go.

Sprinkle coriander and dot with a little butter between layers.

Roll out the top brush bottom and top with egg glaze, place top on bottom and press firmly down to stick it well.

Trim off excess pastry - roll out again and use to decorate top of pie with leaves and berries – pierce a hole in the middle to allow the steam to escape.

Glaze with egg wash and bake for 30-35mins.

Mix the eggs and crème fraîche together in a jug. Season with salt and pepper.

Take the pie out of the oven at the end of the cooking time and with a funnel slowly pour the egg and crème fraîche in the steam hole.

Continue to cook for a further 20-25mins.

Serve hot or warm

Courgette and blue cheese quiche

**1 quantity of basic
   shortcrust pastry made
   with 1 generous tsp of
   aromatic salt**
**3 courgettes cut into very
   fine slices using a
   vegetable peeler to create
   ribbons**
**½ onion, chopped and
   cooked in a knob of
   butter until transparent
   – leave to cool**
5 eggs
250ml milk
500g crème fraîche
**200g blue cheese – if using
   roquefort watch out when
   seasoning with salt as it is
   very salty**
1tbsp chopped tarragon
**sea salt and freshly ground
   black pepper**
2tsp smooth Dijon mustard

Roll out pastry and line loose bottomed quiche tin. Chill in fridge for 30mins without trimming pastry.

Preheat oven to 220°C, 425°F.

Take out pastry and trim to size. Prick with fork and spread the mustard over the base of the pastry or use a home made pesto.

Spread the onions over the base and then the courgettes and dot over the cheese.

In a bowl whisk together with a fork the eggs, crème fraîche and milk – season with salt, pepper and the tarragon. Pour over courgettes – bake until lightly golden and slightly risen – approx. 40mins.

Tarts
Sweet

"O blessed man,
favored by all the
divinities! Eat, give
thanks, and go forth,
'in apple-pie order."

Henry Ward Beecher

Last year my neighbour, who has devoted his entire garden to growing organic fruit and vegetables, had the most enormous glut of red and black currants. So every day I was invited round to pick as many as I could, which, of course, I did willing as I was re-landscaping the garden last year and it looked very similar to a landfill site as 20 trucks of soil were removed.

I was looking for inspiration and discovered, in an old classic French cook box, a wonderful recipe for a custard tart with redcurrant topping glazed with red currant jelly.

It was a huge hit and whilst I still managed to fill the freezer up with juicy red berries, there was also enough to top up the redcurrant jelly stock and make coulis for sorbets. Ditto for black currants and raspberries.

I'd say if I had to choose between chocolate or lemon, lemon would win hands down every time, especially a deep sharp lemon tart. Nothing better for cleansing the palette and ideal after a heavy stew.

A small slice of rich dark chocolate tart, dusted with a flutter of icing sugar served with coffee is also a combination that cannot be ignored.

The versatility of tarts are extensive, and I must admit to being a huge supporter of traditional fruit pies with lids on. There is nothing nicer than a fluffy apple pie with a hint of ground cinnamon and vanilla custard or steamed suet red plum and ginger pie simmering away in a double boiler for hours. Who can resist strawberry tarts fresh from the French patisserie filled with lashings of creamy filling and shiny red glaze, completely irresistible. Tiny little mire belle plums slightly caramelized as they have cooked.

The sweet pastry dough is wonderfully crisp eaten just on its own as a small sablé biscuit with coffee. Simply grate the zest of a small lemon to add a little extra. Using slightly different ingredients can also change the purpose of a sweet tart. A finer more buttery pastry dough is ideal for a crisp shell perfect with light fruit tarts such as strawberries or red currants, and a more sturdy yet crisp sweet crust made with added ground almonds is better when holding a liquid tart that needs cooking in the oven until set.

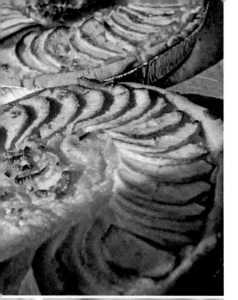

Whatever and however you choose to make a sweet tart, it will be delicious. Chilling before rolling is one of the keys to succeeding with this more delicate dough, so be a little more patient than for a savoury pie or tart. I even freeze for a short time once the tart is lined and defiantly leave excess pastry draped over the edge as shrinkage does occur. Trimming off the edges half way through cooking will ensure the perfect finish. Remember if you are creating a fruit tart to be generous. Pile up the tart and have it full to nearly over flowing. Spoon over a clear, apricot or red glaze and decorate with fresh mint or verbena leaves. Sprinkle over a few drops of rose or orange water just before serving to create the essence of summer!

Redcurrant flan tart

sweet pastry
250g plain flour
45g ground almonds
130g butter
100g icing sugar
1 egg
or see p.71

flan filling
3 eggs
340ml cream
½ vanilla pod, scraped
100g sugar

redcurrant topping
350g redcurrants
2ssp redcurrant jelly

In a food processor add all the ingredients apart from the egg. Blitz for a few moments until it forms fine breadcrumbs. Add the egg and pulse the mixture until it forms a ball. Turn out onto a floured surface, roll into a ball, wrap in clingfilm and chill for 1hr.

Roll out pastry and line tart tin, rectangular, round, square, individual – prick the base with a fork - line with baking parchment and fill the tin with baking beans. Preheat oven to 200°C, 400°F, bake until the edges are golden, then take off the baking parchment with the baking beans on. Return the tart cases to the oven and continue to cook for another 5mins until the base starts to colour.

Mix up the cream, eggs, sugar and vanilla, pour in the pastry mould and return to the oven. Cook the filling for approx. 30mins, in preheated oven 180°C, 350°F. Cool.

Take the red currants off the stalks. Melt 2tsps of redcurrant jelly with a little water, mix well and pour over the redcurrants. Arrange the redcurrants on the cooled custard tart.

Lemon tart and fruits of the forest coulis

600g sweet shortcrust pastry
  (see p.71)
6 lemons, zest and juice
9 free range eggs
350g caster sugar
325ml whipping cream
800g frozen or fresh red
  fruits of the forest
2 tbsp icing sugar
juice of 1 lemon

For the coulis, mix the red fruits of the forest with the icing sugar and juice of 1 lemon – leave for 1hr and then blend until smooth – sieve and reserve. Roll out the pastry and line a buttered tart tin, leaving the excess pastry hanging over the edge – chill in the freezer for 30mins.

Pre-heat oven to 200°C, 400°F. In a large mixing bowl break the eggs in and add the sugar – beat lightly until smooth. Add the cream, lemon juice and zest to the eggs – stir until smooth. Chill.

Line the pastry case with foil or baking parchment and baking beans. Bake for 20 mins until lightly coloured – trim off excess pastry with a sharp knife to create a straight edge that has not shrunk. Stir the lemon mixture and pour into the tart case. Bake for 40 mins until the lemon mixture becomes firm.

Leave to cool and serve with a spoonful of coulis around the plate – decorate with fresh raspberries, strawberries and fresh mint leaves.

White chocolate and raspberry tartlets

12 individual sweet pastry tartlets already made and cooked
150g fresh raspberries, crushed
400g chopped white chocolate
50g melted butter
250ml double cream
1 jar homemade or good quality raspberry jam
1tsp rose water

Heat the cream up in a medium sized saucepan. When it comes to a simmer pour over the chopped white chocolate and melted butter. Stir until the chocolate has melted to form a ganache.

In the bottom of each case spread a spoon of raspberry jam. Pour in the cooled chocolate ganache. In the bowl of crushed raspberries stir in a spoonful of rose water. Place a small spoonful of the raspberry mixture on the top of each tartlet and swirl with the tip of a sharpe knife.

Chill the tarts for an hour or two until set. Remove 15mins before serving.

Serve with a swirl of raspberry mix on the plate.

Tarte Tatin

8 apples, cooking or cox's
1tbsp lemon juice
rind of 2 limes plus juice
grated ginger approx. 5cm
140g butter
250g sugar
300g sweet pastry (see p.71)

Preheat the oven to 220°C, 425°F.

Peel, core and half the apples and put in a bowl with the lemon juice and lime juice, toss gently to coat.

In a large shallow oven proof pan melt the sugar with a little water, when it has caramelized add the butter and slowly stir like crazy to homogenize the caramel. Add the lime rind and the ginger. Stir.

Take the apples halves and pack tightly together sideways up, brush with a little melted butter and bake in the oven for 20mins until they start to soften.

Roll out the pastry on a floured surface approx. 3mm thick. Place over the apples allowing an overlap of 4cm.

Make a thicker border around the dish using this over lap of pastry, place the whole dish back in the oven for 20mins until the pastry is golden.

Take the tart out, leave to rest for 10mins before inverting onto the serving plate, be very careful it will be very, very hot!

Serve with a creamy home made ice cream or fromage blanc ice cream or just thick cream!

Desserts

"If you're afraid of butter, use cream."

Julia Child

The only time I take the trouble to measure ingredients precisely is when I'm baking and making desserts. With most other recipes for salads, main courses and soups as long as there isn't too much seasoning used it's easier to add an inch of this or that, swap ingredients around or opt for other herbs etc.

To achieve a delicious morsel of heavenly loveliness you need to concentrate a little harder.

I definitely recommend reading through the recipe several times and absolutely get all your ingredients together before you start and *always* make it before if it is for an important occasion.

Some recipes call for the use of gelatin other for chilling time in the fridge or freezer, so make sure you have allowed enough time when you are planning.

Strangely enough, many European countries don't really eat dessert on a daily basis, as the English tend to do. It's more cheeses and fruit with something delicious at the weekend but usually bought from a patisserie. Is it because they can't be bothered with all the fuss or is it just because the patisseries make such amazing gâteau there's no point?

Of course, you don't have to go all out with fancy French gâteau unless you want to. There are lots of easier, delicious recipes to enjoy and they are far less stressful. Guests and family will love them whatever type you choose to do. You don't have to be a Goddess to bring happiness into people's lives, just a simple warm chocolate fondant will do nicely. There is something wonderfully comforting about English desserts and I do just love the effect that it has on loved ones. I think it must be the security and bliss of childhood that is evoked by the smell of fresh apple crumble and custard or lemon posset.

It is an unconscious return to the innocence of our youth, carefree days, fun, laughter, sunny days and snowy Christmases before the responsibility of life and washing up took over!

As much as the French patisseries are eye bogglingly spectacular, they don't hold that special place in my heart in the same way as steamed syrup pudding.

Warm cherry batter pudding scented with rose water

2tsp rose flower water
500g cherries, fresh, pitted
8 eggs
pinch of salt
150g plain flour
2tsp baking powder
125g caster sugar or honey
150ml milk
200ml whipping cream
1 vanilla pod, split and
**   scraped out**
25g melted butter
8tsp cherry preserve or
**   compote**

Pre-heat the oven to 200°C, 400°F.

In a large bowl, beat the eggs, vanilla seeds, rose water, sugar or honey, salt and flour.

Gradually pour in the milk, stirring constantly, then add the melted butter. butter your individual dishes or one large dish.

Pour in the batter mixture and arrange the cherries generously in the batter, add a tsp of cherry preserve to each dish.

Bake for approx. 50mins or until the batter is set.

Serve warm with spoons of crème fraîche or vanilla ice cream.

This dessert is also delicious with many other ripe fruits.

Try blackberries with a swirl of redcurrant jelly - Delicious!

Lemon shortbread with strawberries and passion fruit

1kg strawberries, washed, hulled and cut in half if necessary

1 quantity sweet shortcrust pastry (see p.71)

3 passion fruits, cut in half, juice and seeds scraped out

1 quantity fruits of the forest coulis

35g icing sugar

250g mascarpone

1 vanilla pod scraped out

20g icing sugar for the mascarpone

vanilla essence

Preheat oven to 180°C, 350°F.

In a blender add all the pâté sablée ingredients except the egg yolks and lemon essence.

Blend to form bread crumbs then add the egg yolks and lemon essence.

Blend until it forms smooth dough and chill for a good hour. Mix half the quantity of fruits of the forest coulis with the strawberries and passion fruits, Chill in the fridge for 30mins.

Mix the mascarpone with the vanilla seeds and sugar Divide the pastry in two.

Roll out both halves and cut out 12 circles.

Bake on a baking tray lined with baking parchment until lightly golden in colour. Leave to cool on a wire rack.

Put a sablée base on a large serving platter or on individual plates, carefully spoon on a small quantity of mascarpone cream and some strawberries and passion fruits.

Add another sablée, more mascarpone cream and the rest of the strawberries and passion fruit. Place the last sablée on top on the fruits and dust with icing sugar.

Serve the remaining coulis in a jug or spoon around the plates. These can also be made as individual desserts.

Lemon posset with lemon curd and shortbread

600ml double cream
135g sugar
4 lemons, juice and rind
1 jar of home made lemon curd
1 quantity of shortbread dough (see p.71)
1 tub mascarpone cheese
small punnet of blueberries
3tsp sugar
1 vanilla pod scraped out
mint leaves to decorate (optional)

Pour cream and sugar into a large saucepan and boil for 3mins. Whisk in the lemons and strain.

Put ½tsp of lemon curd in the base of each serving pot and gently pour the cream in. Chill until they have set, approx. 4hrs.

Roll out the shortbread dough to 3mm. Using a fluted pastry cutter cut out small circles approx. 3cm diameters. Carefully place on a lined baking sheet and bake in a moderate oven until they just start to colour. Remove and leave to cool on a wire rack.

In a bowl turn out the mascarpone, add the vanilla seeds and sugar. Mix well.

Pipe a small amount onto half the shortbread discs.

Sit 4-5 blueberries on top and place a 2nd shortbread disc on top. Dust with icing sugar.

To serve
On your chosen plate place a pot of lemon cream and next to it a shortbread biscuit with mascarpone and blueberries

Chocolate fondant

**500g plain good quality
chocolate
230g butter
8 large free range eggs +
2 extra yolk
pinch of salt
230g caster sugar
1 vanilla pod scraped out
45g plain flour**

Place the individual pudding basins in the freezer for 1hr then grease with softened butter (not melted).

Line with a circle of baking parchment and butter. Dust with flour and return to the freezer.

In a double boiler, melt the chocolate and butter. Cool slightly.

Whisk up the eggs, extra yolks, fresh vanilla, pinch of salt and sugar until pale and fluffy.

Loosen up the cooled chocolate with a little of the egg mixture and then gradually but swiftly fold in the rest, sprinkle the flour over the top and briskly but carefully fold in 3-4 strokes.

Spoon into the pudding basins approx. just over ½ way up. Chill for as long as possible or freeze.

Oven to 200°C, 400°F gas 6.

If chilled in fridge bake for 15mins until firm on the top but wobbly when you touch. If frozen cook for 20mins, but keep checking take out when firm on top but wobbly when you touch.

Remember they will carry on cooking when you take them out of the oven.

Leave to rest for 5mins. Swiftly turn upside down onto serving plate, remove tin and circle of baking parchment.

Dust with icing sugar and serve with vanilla crème fraîche, warm chocolate sauce or vanilla ice cream.

SHOP. COOK. EAT.

Rhubarb and apple charlotte

**40 slices of stale white bread
  or brioche**
soft butter
1kg rhubarb
100g butter
150g sugar
7 crispy apples

**12 pudding basins well
  buttered or 2 cake tins**

Heat oven to 180°C, 350°F.

Cut discs to fit the bases and the tops of the pudding basins or tins.

Cut 3cm slices out of the rest of the bread, crusts removed.

Butter 1 side and place butter side down in the tins, overlapping slightly.

Peel, if necessary, the rhubarb and cut into cubes.

Melt half the butter in a large pan.

Add the rhubarb once the butter is bubbling. Add half the sugar. Cook for 5mins then strain and collect juice for later. Repeat the process with the apples, but no need to strain.

Keep a little of each fruit to one side.

Mix the 2 fruits together, taste and sweeten if necessary. Divide the mixture between the pudding basins, top with the lids and fold over the excess bread.

Cook in a pre heated oven. Individual desserts take 20mins to cook – large 45mins.

Whilst the charlottes are cooking blend the set aside fruit with the collected rhubarb juice, strain and use to serve as a coulis.

Turn out the charlottes and serve with extra thick double cream and coulis. The charlottes should be crispy.

Mocha and white chocolate baked cheesecake

300g double chocolate chip cookies
90g melted butter
500g melted white chocolate
500g low fat cream cheese
5 eggs
100g plain chocolate, chopped
4tsp instant coffee
100ml double cream
extra 50g dark and white chocolate grated or curled for decorations

Preheat oven to 150°C, 300°F.

Grease the loose bottom cake tin, dariole moulds or stainless steel rings and line with greaseproof paper.

If you are using small coffee cups you don't need to.

In a food processor, grind up the biscuits to make crumbs. Mix with the melted butter and divide the mixture between the moulds. Make a firm base with the back of a spoon.

Mix the cream cheese with the eggs until smooth. Mix in the white chocolate.

Mix the chopped dark chocolate with the instant coffee, and melt with 3tbsps of hot water.

Spoon ⅔ white chocolate mixture into the tins. Dribble the dark chocolate mixture over the white chocolate and with the point of a skewer or a cocktail stick make a few swirls then top with the rest of the white chocolate. Cook for 20mins.

Remove from the oven and chill.

Whisk up the cream and top the cheesecakes with a blob.

Grate the dark and white chocolate over the top and serve with a small cookie or just single cream.

coffee cups, dariole moulds or small stainless steel rings if you want to make individual cheesecakes or a large loose bottom cake tin

Crêpe suzette, façon Gregoire

for the crêpe
500ml milk
150g flour
4 eggs
a pinch of salt
1tbsp veg oil

for the suzette
100g sugar
50g butter
200ml fresh orange juice
100ml fresh grapefruit juice
50ml fresh lemon juice
50ml grand marnier
50ml Cointreau
a splash of Cognac

Mix the eggs, flour and salt together with a whisk until smooth.

Mix in the oil and then gradually pour in the milk and stir until batter is smooth. Allow to stand for 30mins. The crêpe can be made in advance.

In a non stick frying pan heat until hot and 'gregoire says' use half a potato dipped in oil to coat the pan, which is enough to prevent sticking.

Make all the crêpe and cover with a tea towel until needed.

Melt the butter in a large frying pan. Fold the readymade crêpe into six and place into the frying pan. When the crêpe are warm turn over and sprinkle with sugar.

Then pour on all the alcohol and flambé - *Warning big flames no fan!*

When the flames have died down pour on the fruit juices and leave to simmer until juice has reduced by half.

Serve on plate and spoon over excess juice

Charlie's chocolate macaroons

200g icing sugar
180g ground and sifted
    almonds
30g cocoa powder
160g egg white
200g caster sugar

for chocolate ganache
250g dark bitter chocolate
20cl heavy cream
50g butter
½tsp coffee extract
    (optional)

Make the ganache by heating the cream in a saucepan.

Put the chocolate, butter and coffee extract in a bowl.

When it starts to simmer take off the heat and pour over the chocolate, beat until smooth and reserve at room temperature until needed.

For the macaroons
In a food processor blend the icing sugar, cocoa powder and ground almonds until completely fine, then sieve into a clean dry bowl.

In a saucepan (not too big but with a heavy base) add the sugar and water.

Bring to a slow boil and using a sugar thermometer boil until 110°C is reached.

When the sugar reaches 100°C, 200°F, start whisking ½ the egg whites in a large dry, clean bowl.

Remove the sugar from the heat as soon as it reaches 110°C, 210°F wait for the bubbles to stop and then slowly pour into the beaten egg whites in a thin steady stream with the whisk going all the time.

Keep the machine whisking until the meringue is cool/cold, it will take quite some time, so be patient.

While the meringue is cooling mix the almond and icing sugar mix with the remaining egg whites.

Add a spoonful of beaten egg white to the almond coca mix with a wooden spoon or spatula and mix swiftly to loosen.

Then slowly fold in the rest of the meringue.

Fill up a piping bag with a plain nozzle inserted at the base.

On a large baking sheet, lined with silicone paper, pipe out small dots approx. 2cm in diameter and with space in between them.

P.T.O.

Leave to dry out for at least an hour.

Preheat the oven to 145°C, 275°F.

Cook for approx. 15mins, they should be firm and should no longer stick to the silicone paper.

Slide the paper off the baking tray onto a damp tea towel (this will help the macaroons peel off the paper).

Put on a cooling tray.

When completely cool pipe the ganache onto one side of a macaroon and stick a second disc to it

Place on a dish until all are filled and pressed together.

It is a time consuming process, but the results are delicious. Practise makes perfect!

Bread and butter pudding

1 large French stick, thickly
   sliced
200g soft butter
12 eggs
1 vanilla pod, split in half
   lengthways and scrape the
   seeds out
50ml ruby port, tia maria,
   or something similar
1ltr cream
200g sugar
100g sultanas
½ pot of apricot jam

Preheat oven to 180°C, 350°F.

Thickly butter both sides of the bread and arrange in a large buttered tin. The bread should be arranged with the crust facing upwards to give a crunch.

Soak the sultanas in the port.

In a saucepan add the sugar, cream and the vanilla pod split in half with the vanilla seeds scraped out.

Bring the cream to just a simmer, stir and turn off the gas. Leave to infuse for 20mins.

Crack the eggs into a large bowl and whisk in the infused cream.

Sprinkle the sultanas over the bread, poking down and around the sides and between the slices.

Pour over the excess port. Pour over the egg and cream mixture.

Gently press the slices of bread down and bake in the oven in a roasting tray with a little water around it to make a bain-marie, until the egg and cream mixture is set. Approx. 50mins.

Check by gently pressing the bread down.

If the cream and egg mixture oozes out then it isn't quite cooked.

Take out of oven and spoon over jam to form a shiny surface.

Passion fruit and mango mousse gâteau

a stainless steel cake ring or loose bottom tin approx. 20cm diameter

genoise sponge cake
125g sugar
125g flour
4 eggs
20g melted butter

for the mousse
500ml passion fruit juice, either bought as a frozen concentrate that will be slightly sweetened or approx. 30 passion fruits, cut in half, pulp scooped out into a food processor and razzed to release the juice, then strained
500ml mango concentrate or approx. 10 ripe mangoes, pulped and sieved
5 leaves gelatin or use a vegetarian substitute following manufacture's guidelines
4 egg whites
70g sugar
220g whipping cream
raspberries to decorate, fresh flowers, mint leaves etc.

Preheat oven to 200°C, 400°F. In an electric cake mixer whisk the eggs and sugar until really thick, I always write my initial with the whisk on the surface, if it holds its done.

Sift in the flour and carefully fold through the mixture, careful not to knock out the air. Pour in the cooled melted butter.

Stir carefully through and pour into the cake tin. Bake until golden brown and springy to the touch, approx. 20mins. Turn out onto a cooling rack and cool.

Slice the cake carefully in half, horizontally, to make 2 discs. Freeze one for another time or cut out smaller individual circles for left over mixture!

Mix the passion fruit and mango purees together. Moisten the sponge with some juice.

Keep 200ml of the juice aside for the glaze and 100ml for the sauce. In a saucepan reduce down the remaining juice by a third.

Soak 3 of the gelatin leaves in ice cold water for at least 2mins then drain and squeeze the excess water out.

Add to the hot passion fruit and mango purées. Cool rapidly.

Meanwhile whisk up the whipping cream to a soft peak. Whisk up the egg whites gradually adding the sugar until it is softly firm. Carefully fold in the egg whites to the cream and then fold in the passion fruit and mango purées.

Pour into the mould but leave 4mm of room from the top. Chill for at least 6hrs or overnight.

2hrs before serving heat up the 200ml reserved juice and soak the remaining gelatin leaves in ice cold water for 2mins, drain and squeeze out the excess water. Dissolve in the juice and cool.

Carefully spoon over the top of the mousse and chill until set

Using a blow torch very carefully sweep the blowtorch

around the sides of the mousse and gently lift off the mould

I often swap the pouring sauce for a raspberry coulis instead as it adds a different colour that picks out the fresh raspberries on the top of the mousse

TIPS
Different country's have different sized gelatin leaves I have found. In the UK they are half the size of the French ones, so check the amount of gelatin required by volume of liquid.

Decorate with fruits, flowers or both and serve on a pretty plate with the remaining juice in a jug.

Crème Brulée

12 egg yolks
130g runny honey
1 vanilla pod, seeds
   scraped out
800ml cream
300ml milk
1tsp rose water or orange
   flower water or 1tbsp
   lavender flowers
soft brown sugar for the top

Whisk the egg yolks and honey together.

In a saucepan warm the vanilla pods and seeds and lavender flowers (if using) or the vanilla pods and seeds with the rose or orange flower water, with the cream and milk – do not boil just warm through take off the heat and leave to infuse for 30mins.

Strain the pods and lavender flowers out of the milk then whisk gently into the eggs and honey.

Divide the cream between the ramekin dishes or crème brulée dishes.

Place the dishes in a shallow baking tray and surround with hot water until it is halfway up the sides of the dishes.

Transfer to a warm oven – be very careful when carrying the baking tray that the water does not spill out on your hands.

Bake until the cream is almost firm when gently shaken approx. 45mins in a low oven 120°C, 250°F.

Transfer the crème to the fridge and chill for several hours.

Just before serving sprinkle the tops of the crème evenly with brown sugar and safely melt the sugar with a blow torch.

If it catches and starts to ignite – Don't panic just blow it out.

If all the sugar is not quite melted but the other side is, stop and go on to the next crème and come back to it afterwards, this will avoid it igniting on the side that is already melted!

Baking

"The nice thing about baking alone in the kitchen before dawn is that you can talk to yourself like a crazy person"

William Alexandrer

If I was asked what is my most favourite thing to do, I think I'd have to say baking.

It's such a hard choice to make because if you spend many days baking and decorating, which I still do, it can wane a little and I crave to make a beef stew, but in the end I find baking, bread and pastry making so rewarding.

What I do find a shame is that some desserts and cakes can take many hours to make but by the end of the meal everyone is totally stuffed, and pass in favour of a small slither of cheese. I know, I am one of those people!

Or, it looks so good to eat, they don't eat it! We are our own worst enemy, but once the first slice goes, the rest quickly follows.

Actually I don't have a sweet tooth, but I love what I love and that's a good slice of excellent cake from time to time. My favourite being the simplest, a freshly made lemon drizzle cake or coffee and walnut just like my Grannie used to make. That warm squishy chocolate cake with freshly made butter cream that is slightly shiny because the cake is still a little warm - gone in five! I like what it means to people and how it can, served at the right time of day make us sit down and just relax for a moment.

Cooking for a very impressive Russian client one day a while ago in this exquisite Chateau, deep in the heart of Burgundy, where things were obviously not going the way the host had planned, I proceeded to unpack my ingredients. Quickly followed by an all in one coffee and walnut cake from Grannie's archives, placed it on the table with a pot of tea and let the aroma of freshly baked cake draw people to the kitchen.

The musicians, fresh in from St Petersburg, and the Russian host from totally different ends of the social spectrum then proceeded to devour the cake and drink pots and pots of tea, with much laughter and song.

Tea time treats

one quantity sweet
   shortcrust pastry dough
   (see p.71)
300g mascarpone
100ml double or whipping
   cream
1ssp icing sugar
1tbsp good quality lemon
   curd or homemade lemon
   curd (it's so easy to make,
   you'll never look back!)
the seeds from ½ a fresh
   vanilla pod
extra icing sugar for dusting
blueberries to decorate

sweet shortcrust pastry
with almonds
300g plain flour
60g ground almonds
zest of one lemon
125g butter
125g icing sugar
2 eggs

for the filling
6 lemons, zest & juice
9 free range eggs
350g caster sugar
325ml whipping cream
peel of 1 lemon, pith
   removed and sliced into
   fine julienne
extra sugar

For the lemon shortbread biscuits with blueberries
Preheat oven to 180°C, 350°F.

Roll out gently onto a floured surface and using a fluted or flower shaped pastry cutter cup out 3-4cm shapes. Cut out enough to have tops and bottom. Cook until the colour is just appearing around the edges.

Whisk up all the other ingredients until firm but not too stiff. Take out and cool. Using a teaspoon put a generous amount in the middle of the biscuit and gently press to the edges. Decorate with blueberries.

Take the top biscuit and put a small amount of lemon cream in the middle and then gently press down being careful not to crush the filling. Dust the top lightly with the extra icing sugar.

Lemon tart
In a food processor add all the ingredients apart from the egg. Blitz for a few moments until it forms fine breadcrumbs.

Add the eggs and pulse the mixture until it forms a ball. Turn out onto a floured surface, roll into a ball, wrap in clingfilm and chill for 45mins. You can freeze it at this stage.

Roll out the pastry and line a buttered tart tin, leaving the excess pastry hanging over the edge – chill in the freezer for 30mins or use individual moulds.

Pre-heat oven to 200°C, 400°F.

In a large mixing bowl break the eggs in and add the sugar – beat lightly until smooth. Add the cream, lemon juice and zest to the eggs – stir until smooth. Chill.

Roll out the pastry and line the pastry case with foil or baking parchment and baking beans. Bake for 20mins until lightly coloured – trim off excess pastry with a sharp knife to create a straight edge that has not shrunk.

Stir the lemon mixture and pour into the tart case. Bake for 40mins until the lemon mixture becomes firm. Leave to cool.

Blanch lemon julienne in boiling water, refresh in cold water and repeat. After the 2nd time return to pan with 1 tbsp sugar and 2 tbsp water, simmer until syrupy. Use to decorate the top of the tarts.

225g sugar
275g self-raising flour,
  sieved
1 tsp baking powder
225g butter, soft
splash of milk
6 fresh free range eggs
zest and juice of 3 lemons
extra 80g sugar for topping
100g icing sugar

For the double lemon drizzle cake

Enough for 2 round tins, 2 loaf tins or 2 brownie tins, grease and line. Preheat oven to 200°C, 400°F.

If you are in a rush make an all in one cake and add 1 tsp extra baking powder. If not make in the traditional way.

Whisk butter, lemon zest from 2 lemons and sugar together until pale and fluffy, scraping down the bowl on several occasions to make sure it is all well combined. Whisk the eggs together with a fork in a jug, you should aim to get big fat bubbles – remember the more air you can incorporate the lighter the cake.

Reduce the speed on the mixer and gradually add the egg, whisk with fork before adding again. If you see the cake is slightly on the edge of curdling, add a small amount of flour. When all the egg is in, turn off machine and fold in sieved flour. Add the juice of one lemon and a splash of milk, fold through gently.

Divide between tins, or use a loaf tin or brownie tin. Cook until golden and well risen.

Syrup in a saucepan, add the extra sugar and lemon juice, simmer until syrupy. Cool.

When cake comes out of oven, prick with skewer and spoon over lemon syrup, reserving 1 tbsp. Cool and remove from tin.

Mix icing sugar with reserved lemon syrup to form a thick, but still able to pour paste. Spoon over cake.

Special toffee brownies

for the toffee
50g unsalted butter
150g sugar

for the cookies
400g unsalted butter
570g plain flour
1tsp salt
500g good quality dark
   chocolate, either chopped
   or bought as small
   buttons
4 free range eggs
450g sugar
1 vanilla bean, scraped
80g ground almonds

Preheat the oven to 170°C, 325°F.

Line a tray with foil ready for the toffee.

In a heavy bottomed pan melt the butter and sugar over
a medium heat, stirring constantly. Stir until it turns a dark
caramel colour, it will split, but keep stirring vigorously and
it will come back into a caramel.

Pour into the prepared foil lined baking tray and cool. Brush
a brownie tray with butter, or spray.

Sift the flour and salt into a bowl with the ground almonds.
Melt the chocolate and butter over a pan of simmering water.

Whisk the eggs sugar and vanilla together. Stir in the butter and
chocolate mixture. Then add the flour, salt and almond mix.

Break the toffee into small pieces and add to the brownie mix.

Pour the mixture into the tin and bake for approx. 25mins.
Cool completely before removing from the tin. Cut into
squares or rectangles.

*Can be warmed through and served with chocolate or toffee
sauce with vanilla icecream.*

Chocolate pecan muffins

*makes 12 fancy muffins,
14-16 normal sized muffins.*

400g self-raising flour
2tsp baking powder
150g ground almonds
2 large free range eggs
320g caster sugar
150g melted, unsalted
   butter
350ml milk
200g melted dark chocolate
100g chopped pecan nuts
icing sugar to dust

Preheat oven to 190C, 375°F.

Get the muffin tins ready with some paper muffin cases.

In one bowl add the flour, baking powder, ground almonds.
In another bowl whisk sugar, eggs and melted butter, and
chocolate. Stir through the chopped pecan nuts.

Then add all the dried ingredients to the wet mix. Stir swiftly
in sweeping movements until it is just about mixed, but still
has lumps. Don't over mix, you're not making a cake.

Spoon into muffin cases, and bake for 25-30mins.

Cranberry compote and mango muffins

makes 12 fancy muffins,
14-16 normal sized muffins

400g self-raising flour
2tsp baking powder
150g ground almonds
2 large free range eggs
320g caster sugar
150g melted, unsalted
   butter
350ml milk
zest of 1 lemon or 1 lemon
   and lime
1tsp grated ginger
   (optional, but great if
   using lime zest)
1 ripe mango
300g cranberry compote -
   300g cranberries heated
   with 2tbsp sugar, zest and
   juice of 1 orange, 40ml
   water, until the fruit starts
   to pop, then mash with
   wooden spoon to make
   a pulpy mixture

Preheat oven to 190°C.

Get the muffin tins ready with some paper muffin cases.

In one bowl add the flour, baking powder, lemon zest, ground almonds.

In another bowl whisk sugar, eggs and melted butter, stir through the mango then add all the dried ingredients to the wet mix. Stir swiftly in sweeping movements until it is just about mixed, but still has lumps.

Don't over mix, you're not making a cake.

Spoon into muffin cases, and add a spoon full of cranberry compote, swirl with the point of a thin sharp knife and bake for 25-30mins.

Rhubarb, orange and polenta crumble cake with rhubarb purée

1kg rhubarb, topped,
   tailed, chopped into
   2.5cm lengths
100g caster sugar
rind and juice of 1 orange

cake
200g butter
250g caster sugar
3 free range eggs
125g polenta flour
50g rice flour
1tsp baking powder
125g ground almonds
zest and juice of 1 orange

topping
2tbsp golden caster sugar
2tbsp toasted almonds

Bake rhubarb for 10mins in the oven with the sugar and orange juice, 200°C, 400°F. Cool.

In a food processor add the cake ingredients and mix quickly for 30secs.

Spoon a layer of cake mixture into the base of deep cake tin or loaf tin, then top with rhubarb then more cake mixture.

Bake for 30-45mins depending on the tin size and shape, until the top starts to go a golden brown.

Use the remaining rhubarb to make a syrup for the topping and sprinkle with toasted almonds and a spoon of ice cream or Greek yoghurt.

Almond and orange cake

500g blanched almonds
450g golden caster sugar
130g self raising flour
500g soft butter
2.5tbsp orange zest
8 free range eggs
100g toasted flaked almonds
   to sprinkle on the top
   if you can bare it, melt
   4tbsp of sugar in a pan
   until it starts to
   caramelise, take off the
   heat and tip in the toasted
   flaked almonds, cover and
   tip out onto a grease proof
   sheet on a baking tray.
   When they are cool
   sprinkle over the cake,
   they will be deliciously
   crunchy and will
   doubtlessly get stuck in
   your teeth! Sorrry

orange syrup
150ml freshly squeezed
   orange juice
120g golden caster sugar

Preheat oven to 200°C , 400°F.

Blitz the almonds in a food processor until finely chopped but still slightly crunchy.

Transfer to a mixing bowl and cream in the sugar and flour.

In a separate bowl, beat the butter and orange zest together, then add the eggs one at a time, beating well between each one. Add the almond mixture, mix well and turn out into a greased baking tin. Bake until golden brown.

Take out, leave in the baking tin and prick all over with a fork or knife.

Whilst the cake is baking dissolve the sugar and orange juice together in a saucepan.

Pour over cake and sprinkle over the toasted flaked almonds.

Cool and serve in slices with cream or just on its own.

Blueberry and apple crumble muffins

makes 12 fancy muffins,
14-16 normal sized muffins

400g self-raising flour
2tsp baking powder
150g ground almonds
2 large free range eggs
320g caster sugar
150g melted, unsalted
butter
350ml milk
zest of 1 lemon or 1 lemon
and lime
1tsp grated ginger (optional,
but great if using lime
zest)
1 sour apple peeled, cored
and diced
350g blueberries

crumble
any crumble mix recipe
you have
I use
350g flour
100g sugar
200g butter
rub to form breadcrumbs
store in an airtight container
and keep in fridge or freeze

Preheat oven to 190°C, 375°F.

Get the muffin tins ready with some paper muffin cases.

In one bowl add the flour, baking powder, lemon zest, ground almonds.

In another bowl whisk sugar, eggs and melted butter, stir through the fruits add then add all the dried ingredients to the wet mix. Stir swiftly in sweeping movements until it is just about mixed, but still has lumps.

Don't over mix, you're not making a cake.

Spoon into muffin cases, top with lashings of crumble mix and bake for 25-30mins.

Buttermilk scones

450g self-raising flour, sifted
100g butter, soft
100g caster sugar
2tsp baking powder, sifted
pinch of salt
2 free range eggs, lightly
  beaten
250ml buttermilk
extra flour

Preheat oven to 220°C, 425°F.

Line baking sheets with good quality greaseproof paper.

Rub butter into sieved flour quickly.

With a fork mix in sugar and salt. Whisk the eggs and buttermilk together with a fork. Mix into the flour little by little, you might not need to use it all or you may need to add a bit more.

Knead quickly but lightly. Turn out onto a floured board and roll or pat with fingers to form a thick even base approx. 2cm in thickness.

Cut out with pastry cutters the size you want or just cut into wedges. Place on baking tray and bake for 10-15mins until the tops are golden crispy brown.

Cool on a baking rack.

Serve sliced in half with delicious home made jams and cream.

They can be frozen.

Chocolate fudge cake

800g plain flour
500g vanilla infused caster
  sugar
200g soft light brown sugar
135g cocoa powder,
  unsweetened
5tsp baking powder
2tsp bicarbonate of soda
1tsp salt
6 large fresh free range eggs
250ml sour cream or crème
  fraîche
1tsp vanilla essence or 1 pod
  scraped out
250ml veg oil
600ml milk

fudge icing
400g melted chocolate
1tsp vanilla essence
350g soft butter
600g icing sugar sifted

Pre-heat oven to 190°C, 375°F.

Line your chosen tins.

Whisk the eggs, sour cream and vanilla essence (if using) together until blended – set aside.

Melt butter and cool slightly, blend in the mixing bowl with the oil, then add the chilled water.

Add all the remaining dry ingredients into a large bowl, mix lightly with a fork to distribute the baking powder, salt and bicarb evenly. Pour the whole lot into the oil and butter mix on a slow setting.

Mix until smooth then, add the egg and sour cream mix Pour into tins and bake for approx. 1hr 15mins – after 45mins turn the oven down to 170°C, 325°F – trust your judgement with your own oven – you know how it works best, so these oven instructions are a guide only.

Take out, cool in tin for 20mins and tip onto cooling rack.

fudge icing
Cream butter, vanilla and icing sugar together until very light and fluffy, add the chocolate and spread over cake.

Leftovers

"The most remarkable thing about my mother is that for thirty years she served the family nothing but leftovers. The original meal has never been found."

Calvin Trillin

Just a last few words about leftovers. There is nothing wrong with eating leftovers. It's part of the respect I have for using up all of the bits and bobs that we have worked so hard to produce. Creating a frittata with the bits left in the fridge, no good for a salad, but great pan fried and made into something solid with potatoes and eggs.

Soup, it's a Monday lunch special in our house after the Sunday dinner!

Pop cakes, yes the cake crumbs, can be mixed with butter cream and jam, frozen briefly rolled into balls and dipped in melted chocolate before smothering with sprinkles. Ask the younger generation if they would mind eating that! I don't think there will be too many 'no's.

Stale bread gets turned into crumbs and frozen until needed.

The cheese mountain in the box at the bottom of the fridge all gets grated up and used in quiche, 'quiche de la fromage perdu' literally translated means quiche of the lost cheese!

Or it can be made into a fondue, macaroni cheese, cheese straws or Kim's special cheese biscuits.

So, waste not, want not!

Conversion table

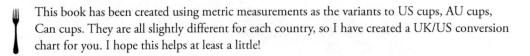

This book has been created using metric measurements as the variants to US cups, AU cups, Can cups. They are all slightly different for each country, so I have created a UK/US conversion chart for you. I hope this helps at least a little!

Oven temperatures

°C	°F
140	275
150	300
170	325
180	350
190	375
200	400
220	425
230	450
240	475

Liquids

Metric	Imperial
5ml	1tsp
15ml	1tbsp
25ml	1fl oz
50ml	2fl oz
100ml	3½fl oz
150ml	5fl oz or ¼pt
200ml	7fl oz
250ml	9fl oz
300ml	10fl oz or ½pt
350ml	12fl oz
400ml	14fl oz
450ml	16fl oz
500ml	18fl oz
575ml	20fl oz or 1pt
1 litre	1 ¾pt

English American translations

Coriander	Cilantro
Aubergine	Eggplant
Seram wrap	Cling film
Courgette	Zucchini

Cups, grams and ounces

I have rounded them up to an even number because it drives me crazy to have all the decimal points.

Flour and sugar

Cups	Grams	Ounces
⅛c	15g	.55oz
¼c	35g	1.10oz
⅓c	45g	1.5oz
½c	65g	2.25oz
¾c	95g	3.4oz
1c	130g	4.5oz

Bread flour

¼c	35g	1.2oz
⅓c	45g	1.6oz
½c	70g	2.4oz
1c	140g	4.8oz

Rolled oats

¼c	20g	.75oz
⅓c	30g	1oz
½c	45g	1.5oz
1c	85g	3oz

Packed brown sugar

¼c	55g	1.9oz
⅓c	75g	2.6oz
½c	110g	3.9oz
1c	220g	7.75oz

Honey, molasses, syrup

¼c	85g	3oz
⅓c	115g	4oz
½c	170g	6oz
⅔c	230g	8oz
¾c	255g	9oz
1c	340g	12oz

Index

44268300R00142

Made in the USA
Middletown, DE
02 June 2017